The Instructor's Handbook
for Hilgard, Atkinson, and Atkinson's
INTRODUCTION TO PSYCHOLOGY
SEVENTH EDITION

John C. Ruch

Mills College

HARCOURT BRACE JOVANOVICH, INC.
New York   San Diego   Chicago   San Francisco   Atlanta

ISBN: 0-15-543669-4

Printed in the United States of America

CONTENTS

I. USING THIS HANDBOOK

This handbook recognizes that the introductory psychology course is often taught by new instructors and that it is one of the hardest courses to teach well, even for experienced instructors. Consequently, it has been designed to provide you with as much aid as possible in planning, teaching, and evaluating this course.

New instructors are likely to find it of greatest use, but more experienced instructors may also find it helpful, especially if their experience is primarily with courses other than the introductory one. The handbook is also intended for teaching assistants (TAs); while relatively few comments are addressed directly to them, TAs have been considered as potential readers of all sections.

This volume is called an instructor's "handbook," instead of the more usual "manual," because of the number and variety of specific suggestions included, many of which are not readily available elsewhere. It includes not only the material usually found in an instructor's manual, but also many detailed and practical suggestions for planning and teaching the introductory psychology course, as well as references for further help. Essentially all of this handbook is directed to you. While short-essay questions are included, the multiple-choice questions that make up the primary contents of many instructor's manuals are presented separately in the Test Item File.

Instead of test questions, what you will find here are suggestions for structuring the course (including the use of mastery systems), for lecturing, for testing and grading, for finding and using class supplements (guest lecturers, films, demonstrations, and so on), for supplementary readings (including how to obtain free copies), and for evaluating your course. Some inclusions may seem obvious to experienced instructors. If you are already familiar with the contents of one section, skip it and go on to another.

The general contents of the six major sections are noted below. The table of contents lists them and all subsections, for reference; many of the sections are cross-referenced, to further aid you in finding what you need. (Occasionally, for convenience, sections will include comments similar to those in other sections, but most material is cross-referenced rather than duplicated.)

This section provides a brief introduction. Section II concerns planning the introductory psychology course; it gives details of a typical course, notes the many decisions to be made by you or by others, and describes the resources available to aid you in planning and teaching the course. Section III offers some hints for teaching the introductory course and for handling the many managerial functions often associated with it, including special consideration of discussion sections. Section IV discusses the text, *Introduction to Psychology*, Seventh Edition, and its supplements; it gives the goals and features, noting differences from the Sixth Edition for those of you familiar with it, and suggests ways of using the text and its supplements. Section V considers the evaluation systems that many schools now use; it notes the several and often conflicting purposes they are meant to serve and the types of systems that can be used, both during the course and at the end. Section VI offers some specific chapter-by-chapter teaching supplements: film and lecture/demonstration suggestions and short-essay questions. (As noted above, multiple-choice questions are provided separately; see Section IVD for details.)

The handbook can be either read as a book or used as a reference work. It is strongly recommended, however, that you read at least the remainder of this section and familiarize yourself with the contents so that you know what assistance this handbook can provide when problems occur. Other sections may then be referred to as necessary. If you are new to introductory psychology, and especially if you are new to teaching itself, you will probably find it useful to read also Section II and at least the relevant portions of Sections III and IV. These sections contain useful and practical information rarely provided to new instructors by their departments. If you are already totally committed to specific forms of evaluation, you can omit Section V, but if any choices remain—and some almost certainly do, such as adding other forms of evaluation for particular purposes—it will probably be useful to read Section V when you have the time.

Section VI can be used a chapter at a time. It is likely to be of most use to new instructors but might be helpful even to experienced ones. It is intended to be used as a reference. If you are making up a film list, for example, the chapter-by-chapter specific suggestions of Section VI offer direct help in choosing films. Similarly, Section VI provides chapter-by-chapter suggestions on specific lecture topics or demonstration ideas.

Others have, of course, written at substantially greater length about many of the problems of teaching in general and of teaching the introductory psychology course in particular. Two books by McKeachie are especially helpful and strongly recommended to both instructors and TAs; they are listed below and are referred to occasionally throughout. Other books on teaching are listed in B. Singer's JSAS bibliography noted in Section IIC2. In addition, the American Psychological Association (APA) offers two very useful publications: a comprehensive listing of available resources to aid you in teaching the introductory course and a University of Michigan report on the status of the undergraduate curriculum in psychology (popularly known as the "Red Book" and the "Gray Book," respectively, and referred to by these names throughout). The *Directory of Teaching Innovations in Psychology* can also be useful. These publications are listed below and are described in more detail, together with other offerings of the APA, in Section IIC2.

It is obvious that this handbook cannot build your course for you, much less teach it, but it is the author's hope that it can help provide some of the necessary structural materials for you to build your own course and that it will alert you to some of the problems and possible solutions in the teaching of it.

For further suggestions, see:

American Psychological Association. (1973) *The Psychology Teacher's Resource Book: First Course* (the "Red Book"). Washington, D.C.: APA

Kulik, J. A., and others. (1973) *Undergraduate Education in Psychology* (the "Gray Book"). Washington, D.C.: APA.

Maas, J. B., and Kleiber, D. A. (eds.) (1975) *Directory of Teaching Innovations in Psychology.* Washington, D.C.: APA.

McKeachie, W. J. (1969) *Teaching Tips: A Guidebook for the Beginning College Teacher* (6th ed.). Lexington, Mass.: Heath.

Walker, E. L., and McKeachie, W. J. (1967) *Some Thoughts About Teaching the Beginning Course in Psychology.* Belmont, Calif.: Brooks/Cole.

II. PLANNING THE INTRODUCTORY PSYCHOLOGY COURSE

A. CHARACTERISTICS OF THE TYPICAL INTRODUCTORY PSYCHOLOGY COURSE

1. Heterogeneity of Students. One of the major sources of difficulty in planning and teaching the typical introductory psychology course is the heterogeneity of students. They often differ widely in numerous crucial characteristics, including their backgrounds, their reasons for taking the course, and their abilities.

If freshmen are permitted to take the course, the problems increase. Freshmen are likely to be deficient in many of the skills needed for the typical omnibus introductory course. They have trouble with the amount of reading, taking exams, and writing papers. They often don't know very much about themselves, the school, or your course. Typically they have been selected from the top fraction of their high school grading curve and must adjust to a whole new college curve, one in which half of them will be necessarily in the bottom half. Many of them will be in the class voluntarily, but others will be there under duress, having found introductory psychology listed as a prerequisite for what they really want.

Your problems are not limited to those of the freshmen, however. You will almost certainly also have some older students—perhaps seniors, even graduate students—in other majors, who may know very little about the social sciences, but are very accomplished at studying and taking exams. Some of them may be very good at writing papers but poor at answering multiple-choice questions, whereas others may be the opposite. All of these students, however, will at least have a general orientation to college, and presumably their inexperience will be limited to the specific field of psychology.

In any case, you are well advised to find out the demographics of your particular group as soon as possible. The best way is probably via a brief questionnaire given on the first day of class. Many schools use registration cards that request part of the information you want, such as class and major; you can have students write additional information on the backs of these cards or use other cards. How many questions you ask depends on your ambition, but you should at least have age, class, and major (declared or probable); a list of previous related courses and goals or expectations for the course probably would be useful, too. (For further discussion of the student composition of introductory classes, see the APA's Gray Book.)

2. Multiplicity of Purposes. Another underlying source of difficulty in planning the introductory course is the fact that it typically attempts to serve more purposes than does a more specialized course. It attempts to prepare psychology majors by introducing them to the basic elements of the field (which could be termed "introductory" psychology); at the same time it attempts to provide general knowledge of the field for nonspecialists (which could be termed "general" psychology). Orienting a course specifically to either of these purposes would help determine various aspects of the course—for example, the amount of statistics covered. An "introductory" course would emphasize both the philosophy and methodology of science in general and psychology in particular, including the experimental method and both descriptive and analytical statistics. It would then provide the basic terminology, research history, and orientation to current problems for each of the major subfields. A "general" course, on the other hand, would provide a broad orientation to science and experimentation but would not expect to prepare students to be scientists. In the subfields of psychology, emphasis would fall on important findings and their applications, both to other disciplines and to everyday life.

However, unless you are teaching at a large school where these are offered as distinctly different courses, you will no doubt have students oriented to both purposes. How you reconcile the conflicting approaches implied by these two purposes is one of the general decisions you must make. (These decisions are considered below, in Section IIB. For further discussion, see the APA's Gray Book.)

3. Differences from Other Psychology Courses. If you have taught other psychology courses but not the introductory course, you will find that it poses a whole new set of problems and requires new skills. Most of them flow from the nature of all large introductory or survey courses; some of them have already been elaborated in the preceding two sections: heterogeneity of students and multiplicity of purposes. As an instructor in any such course, you are likely to find that whatever you say will bore some students and confuse others; whatever kind of testing you use will be easier for some students than for others; any approach to the subject will serve some students' purposes at the expense of others; the course will cover topics that some students were not even aware were included, while each topic covered will be too briefly considered for those whose primary interest it is. The best you can do is to compromise, to seek some "golden mean" that you and the students can live with. (This does not imply that a middle-of-the-road approach should be taken for each topic. You may wish to try to mix topics and approaches designed for the two different types, within the course and even within a single meeting.)

If you are more familiar with other courses in psychology, new problems you are likely to encounter in the introductory course include students coerced into the class for an "outside" unit or a prerequisite, often for such fields as sociology or education; upper-level students completely naive about psychology; and freshmen. Furthermore, some of these students will be hostile toward the course, the instructor, or both.

Other problems will include the difficulties of lecturing on nearly all aspects of psychology, those which you have never studied as well as that which is your life work; testing large numbers of students fairly and reliably with a reasonable expenditure of time; managing the experimental-subject pool drawn from this class; or managing one form or another of sections using teaching assistants (TAs).

Instructors accustomed to other courses will thus find themselves busy with support functions, teaching on a more superficial plane, and covering a much broader range of topics. They will be teaching students of widely varying competence, background, and motivation and cannot hope to fit the course to them as effectively as to a selected group of upperclass psychology majors. It is not difficult to understand why the introductory course is often avoided by instructors, if possible, and why it often falls to the beginning instructor. Yet there are also highly capable instructors who find the challenge and the opportunity to excite new students in their own field a continuing source of reward and who teach it regularly. Such instructors note, for example, that the same coverage of many different topics *can* be an advantage; by allowing the instructor to "skim the cream" off various topics, the introductory course can be made more interesting than a more specialized course.

If the introductory course is to be only a temporary way station for you, perhaps this handbook can help you survive and maybe even enjoy it. Who knows? You may even become addicted, seeking to create that better mixture of purposes, that superior elucidation of the scientific method, that gourmet blend of lectures, discussions, films, and demonstrations that will suit the palates of dozens, hundreds, or thousands of young students—giving them a taste of "psychology" that may influence all of their lives.

B. DECISIONS TO BE MADE

1. Your Decisions Versus Others'. In the following subsections, a number of necessary decisions are listed. Only some of them will be yours, however. Some will be specifically given to you, others specifically withheld, while still others will fall in the gray area of "instructor prerogative" or perhaps in the category of "discouraged but allowed." It is important to your understanding of the course's possibilities and conflicts that you recognize what decisions are made, if only by default, and then examine which ones are available to you.

Your primary obligation to your school will be to live up to those responsibilities specifically given to you; for your own sake it is probably best not to try to change strongly entrenched decisions specifically withheld from you. But both you and your school—to say nothing of your students—stand to benefit from a careful consideration of intermediate possibilities.

2. Course Goals. Walker and McKeachie have devoted a chapter of their book (listed at the end of Section I) to the possible goals to be served by the introductory psychology course: (1) communication of elementary concepts; (2) communication of facts; (3) introduction of the full range of the subject matter; (4) integration of the course material; (5) communication of the basic attitudes of the discipline; (6) communication of the intrinsic interest of the subject matter; (7) presentation of the newest developments of the field; (8) provision of individual guidance and monitoring; (9) development of selected intellectual skills; (10) provision of a suitable identification model for the student.

The goals that *you* attempt to achieve via your introductory psychology course will and should be yours, however (even though they may be somewhat limited or influenced by the decisions of others). Furthermore, they should be, if possible, the product of conscious deliberation and choice.

One consideration concerning course goals is whether you wish all students to attempt all the material, with varying degrees of success, or whether you prefer to set some minimal level of knowledge that all students should achieve. If you are interested in the latter, you may wish to consider structuring the entire course along the lines of a "mastery" system such as the "Keller plan." Such systems are discussed in more detail, with references, in Sections IIB10 and IVC.

3. Work and Credit Requirements. The magnitude of your course, in terms of units of course credit, is usually not your decision. In schools where the credit for a course can vary, the introductory psychology course often carries more credit than a usual course, especially if discussion sections or laboratories are included. On the other hand, the amount of work required and its distribution (in terms of exams, papers, or discussion, for example) is usually up to you. Thus, the first caveat is to be sure that the work called for fits the official magnitude of the course.

Your decisions can include a juggling of requirements within the course size, however. If you think that papers are important, perhaps you will want to introduce them in place of an exam. If you want to add outside reading assignments, something else may have to yield to them. It may even be possible for you to add discussion sections where none existed before by giving up one class period a week for their meeting. One way of keeping track of the juggled components is to create a comprehensive course syllabus for distribution to your students, listing all meetings, reading assignments, lecture topics, exams, papers, demonstrations, films, and so on. As suggested in Section IIIA1, such a syllabus may be as useful to you as to your students. Writing out the various class requirements in detail forces you to consider the magnitude and balance of them. In your juggling of course requirements, you will have to consider the weight in grading that each will have. A more detailed discussion of this question is presented in Section IIB10.

These considerations of credit and work requirements have assumed a conventional course structure, with competitive grading, and so on. An alternative is to use a "mastery" system, such as the "Keller plan," in which the work and credit are arranged rather differently. Such systems are discussed in Sections IIB10 and IVC.

4. Experimental-Subject Pool. The traditional research subjects in psychology are the white rat and the college sophomore enrolled in the beginning psychology course. It is probable that as instructor of the basic course you will be responsible for the management of your school's experimental program, if it has one, in addition to more usual teaching duties. With any luck, the details will already have been arranged by others and you will need only to oversee their execution. A specific warning is in order here, however.

It is likely that you will have some range of options for handling the details, but be very careful. Whereas many of the decisions you make about the course will have relatively minor effects, small changes in subject handling can affect such variables as the volunteer rate for particular experiments or the no-show rate for all experiments. Such changes directly affect the research of both faculty and graduate students and if they are changes in the *wrong* direction, you may expect a great deal of unwelcome attention from your colleagues and their students.

Regardless of who makes the decisions, all of the expected protections for subjects need to be provided here, as in all experimentation. As the person in charge, you need to ensure informed consent, privacy of records, and so on, for the entire system, at least insofar as your control of it will allow. (As noted in Section IIC2, the APA publishes a booklet on professional ethics.)

5. Lectures and Guest Lectures. Lectures are, of course, the traditional core of education. The oral transmission of information predates the written word, and in education, other forms of instruction are frequently viewed strictly as supplements to the lecture. But neither lecture nor other forms of instruction can provide passive students with an education. The students' own active involvement is crucial. The important decisions from your point of view concern the choice of techniques for presenting information and for actively involving your students.

Don't let the traditional emphasis on lectures prevent you from a specific appraisal of your own situation. The printed word *does* now exist, complete with illustrations. And slide sets, films, demonstration hardware, TV, and even "multimedia" effects provide more options for information transmission than ever before. So what are you doing standing nervously at a podium, surrounded by clouds of chalk dust, trying to convey information?

In terms of providing students with a package of organized structured information, a good textbook is generally the best system. In terms of vivid involving activity, a well-done film, TV show, or even slide presentation can outperform most lecturers. What, then, can *you* do that they can't?

First of all, you are the organizing force behind all of the above. Some of the organizational decisions to be made have already been noted, and others follow. Section III gives further suggestions for orchestrating these components, and Sections IIB10 and IVC discuss one particular type of course-organization system, the "Keller plan."

But in terms of *lectures*, what can you do? You are *alive*—a real psychologist in the class. This has numerous implications, some of which you might not notice, at least initially. For one thing, the modeling effects can be very powerful. Nothing in the text or audiovisual materials represents "psychology" in the same way that you do. Your interest in the overall field or a particular subfield is easily conveyed and can be very involving for students.

By the same token, your disdain or lack of interest in a subfield of psychology can have very negative effects on your students. And your difficulties in teaching a subtopic in which you are not fully competent—virtually inevitable because of the breadth of introductory psychology—are likely to damage the students' perception of that area of psychology, as well as their view of your abilities and general knowledge.

One way ot handle this latter problem is to call on others as guest lecturers. Members of your own department are the most likely choices, but members of other departments (for example, sociology, linguistics, biology), friends teaching at nearby schools, or even outside professionals (for example, researchers or therapists) may be considered.

Guests should be chosen carefully and both students and guests should be prepared for each other. Guests from your department who have taught introductory psychology will probably need little preparation other than a brief familiarization with what students have and have not covered. If you use an outsider, especially one who has not taught undergraduates regularly, you will need to be sure that the content and level of the presentation will be appropriate for your class. Guests can be very helpful. In addition to covering your weak spots, *they* are also live psychologist models. Just decide whom you will choose and for what particular purpose, keep track of them, and maintain overall control. If you can, the course will offer a lot more to your students.

What else can you do as a live person that other materials cannot? You can sense the knowledge level, current problems, and demands of your students. You can get informal feedback by watching their faces and answering their questions during lectures and by talking to them after class; for more formal feedback you can utilize questionnaires. (See Section VB1.) Being able to sense what your students need and want can be very important, since you are also the person who can respond—by modifying your presentation within a lecture, by choosing topics or guests for later lectures, or by supplementing the course basics with other materials such as films, special demonstrations, or supplementary readings. (See Sections IIB6 and IIB7 for specific suggestions.)

One of the important aspects of this flexibility and response to *your* students' needs offered by the lecture format is the question of what your lecture says—specifically, whether it duplicates text material or ranges a bit afield or covers something completely different. You will probably want to experiment, if you have not already, to find out what you and your students are comfortable with. To some degree, the topic will dictate the treatment. Some topics will be sufficiently important and difficult that you may have to reiterate text material to ensure adequate comprehension; the material on classical and operant conditioning, for example, always seems to be difficult for introductory classes and to need elaboration by the instructor. Other topics will need no such elaboration. For them, you may wish to lecture on applications or implications, to note particular current research details, and so on. (Section IIIA3 and the appropriate portions of Section VI give further suggestions about lecture topics and approaches.)

11

You may also wish to be flexible about the structure of your lectures. The most formal "lecture" presumes no active participation of students, while the notion of a "discussion" or "seminar" presumes a near-equal interaction of students and instructor. "Demonstration" implies the use of the session to present concrete illustrations of concepts. It should be obvious that these types of class structuring (and others, such as films or TV) can be mixed, with one occurring on one occasion, and another, the next.

Various structures can also be readily combined. Even a formal lecture to a large number of students can include student questions, with appropriate modification of your presentation as necessary. Similarly, brief demonstrations, short films, a few slides, or even student discussion among themselves can be advantageously incorporated into a basic "lecture" format.

Most references in this handbook to films or demonstrations will assume that they are the major function of that day's class period, but this is really a simplification of the ideal. Even a film lasting most of the period, for example, can benefit from your comments, student questions, or both. Keep this in mind in reading the handbook and in planning your course, since it offers more options in seeking different goals and allows more flexibility in handling any given class period. Such a mixed format also helps to vary the pace and keep students awake and involved. (Some specific demonstration ideas are included in Section VI; others are included in the APA's Red Book.) Note that various procedures may take more or less time than you expect. Experience is, of course, the best guide, but until you are experienced, you might note that demonstrations and discussion always seem to take more time than you expect, whereas an organized lecture often takes less time. A substantial amount of information is necessary to fill a 50-minute lecture, and finishing in 30 minutes without further notes can be embarrassing. Equally embarrassing can be the effort—which soon becomes obvious—to stretch inadequate material. The best tactic is probably to have more than enough material on each subcategory and use the extra or not as you go along, so that you can fit the material to the time. (If you have to leave out material, don't worry; your students won't miss what they don't have. Just don't try to cram it all in at the end of the hour.)

Thus you have several lecture decisions to make. They can be stated as follows: Decide how many of your class meetings and which topics will be nominally "lectures," as opposed to other uses of time, such as demonstrations, slides, films, or discussion, and why; that is, what purposes are to be served. Once you have planned the major content of your class hours, decide how many of these are suitable for guest lecturers and seek them. Or conversely, if you have willing and capable guest lecturers available, decide where you can best use them. Finally, for your own lectures and as an aid to your guests, decide what relationship to the text each lecture will have and what other elements, if any, it will utilize. In doing this you will be integrating presentation types on two levels. At the first level, your decisions will involve integrating major demonstrations, and so on, into the series of lectures; at the second, they will involve a finer scale of integration, fitting brief demonstrations, and so on, into particular lectures.

6. Films and Demonstrations. As already noted in the discussion on lectures, you must decide what will fill each assigned class hour, seeking the best mix of procedures and content for that ideal course. Demonstrations of psychological phenomena and audiovisual supplements such as slides and 16mm films are the most common alternatives to lectures, although there can be others—for example, videotape. All of them can be used to change the pace, show concrete evidence for theories, and so on. Films have the advantage of transcending time and space, offering the beginning and end of a lengthy experiment in close juxtaposition, a look at events now past and people now dead, or even animation or creation of events that never occurred. Demonstrations, on the other hand, may be more convincing by their immediacy, since students know that filmed "events" are easily created by the film editor. However, any of these can be entertaining without being educational—or at worst be neither.

Sections IIC5, IIC6, and IVE provide you with sources and suggestions for obtaining both information and materials; the chapter-by-chapter listings in Section VI include specific suggestions for appropriate films and demonstrations. This is an area where your colleagues and departmental facilities can be valuable. Even small departments may already own films or demonstration equipment and large ones are virtually certain to; another instructor may be able to provide tips for obtaining and using materials at your particular school.

Thus you need to decide how many films, demonstrations, or other supplements you will use, what they will be, and how they will be fitted into the course. As part of this planning you need to know the sources and any problems in obtaining them. Films, for example, often need to be ordered a semester in advance for showing on a particular date. (See Section IIC5.) In addition, you need to decide details of their role in the class; for example, are you going to provide any prepared passouts and are you going to specifically discuss the material, either before or after its use?

Perhaps most important for your students is whether or not you are going to test them on the material. This factor will influence your students' behavior and may influence your decision to use prepared notes. For example, if you wish to test on a film, remember that it is difficult for students to take legible notes in a darkened room, especially when they are also trying to follow what is going on. A set of prepared notes giving the key points can tell your students both what to look for and what to remember, a situation presumably as desirable from your viewpoint as from theirs. (Note that one benefit of the use of TV in classrooms is that the room need not be completely dark to see it and notes can be taken.)

A final suggestion concerning your decisions on demonstrations is that you consider the probabilities of their failing to work according to plan. (Here especially you may wish to consult others for their experience.) Figure out the advantages you might derive from a failure—for example, evidence of some of the difficulties of doing research or of individual differences across subjects. Balance these advantages and the good effects of success against your embarrassment and loss of face for psychology if you fail, and then decide.

You can, of course, minimize the possibilities of failure by careful preparation and perhaps even a trial rehearsal without observers, preferably in the same room to ensure that sources of power, visual angles, acoustics, and so on, are adequate. This will greatly reduce the probability of failure. It will also give you a better idea of the time involved; running out of time just as you wish to sum up the results is not very helpful to your students, however dramatic the demonstration. (Familiarize yourself with the equipment ahead of time, whether it involves films, tapes, or demonstrations; many class hours have been sacrificed to the frantic pursuit of extension cords and other trivia.)

Lest you feel too cowed by the discussion of problems, however, note that live demonstrations, even of simple phenomena, are very powerful tools. Listening to someone's speech disintegrate with a feedback delay of a fraction of a second says more to the student about the importance of feedback loops than reading or discussion can convey.

7. Supplementary Readings. One aspect of most introductory psychology courses is that they are very broad and cover many topics; some instructors thus limit the coverage to less than all topics covered by the text. Why, then, consider any *supplementary* reading? There are several reasons.

One reason is to emphasize and develop certain areas in courses that do reduce the number of topics covered. Such readings can be designed to cover particular areas in more detail, perhaps including more historical coverage or more details of current research, or perhaps just considering the issues in more depth than is possible in a single text of manageable proportions. (The paperback monograph series listed in Section IIC1 are likely to be particularly useful for these purposes.)

Another reason is to add motivation through readings that may be characterized as more "exciting," "involving," "informal," or "relevant" than the text. Clearly, no text, much less *Introduction to Psychology*, Seventh Edition, sets out to be *not* "exciting," and so on. But a paperback such as Hannah Green's *I Never Promised You a Rose Garden* is nevertheless different from a chapter on abnormal psychology. McCollom has termed such readings "thrillers" ("Psychological Thrillers: Psychology Books Students Read When Given Freedom of Choice." *American Psychologist* 26 (1971): 921–27). The fact that such books are read by choice and are involving for the students not only can serve the immediate purposes of the course but can influence their future reading habits as well. Such "thrillers" may simply be made available to students through a reserve system, but students are not likely to read them without some extrinsic motivation. Assigning short passages or requiring one or more short reports on books (or chapters) of the students' choosing can serve this function.

A third reason, related to that above, is to help the students integrate the text material with other information and other sources. Readings from newspapers or magazines, from the popularized psychology magazines *Psychology Today* and *Human Behavior*, from the professional journals, or from outside but related areas such as sociology, anthropology, ethology, law, and linguistics may be used to put psychology into perspective, both with daily experience and with other disciplines. One way of acquainting students with the professional literature and how to use it is to require them to use *Psychological Abstracts* to find a couple of articles on a topic of their own choosing. (Brief personal reports help ensure that they are read.)

Supplementary readings may also be used in discussion sections (see Sections IIB9 and IIIC3) as a basis for more extensive treatment of specific topics.

Given that there are reasons for supplementary readings, how do you go about deciding what to use when? This is essentially a problem of finding the right books to serve a planned function, or perhaps in some cases of deciding when and how to use a favorite book. The text itself provides lists of supplementary readings for each chapter. (Note that they may be useful to you, in supplementing your knowledge of areas in which you are weak, as well as to your students.) Other sources of readings and suggestions for obtaining them are presented in detail in Sections IIC1 and IIC2.

There are several general categories of supplementary readings to choose from. Perhaps the most general choice is one of the numerous readers specifically designed for introductory psychology—often focusing on particular issues or approaches to psychology and including popular as well as professional articles. (See Section IIC1.) Such readers can be used both for general course supplements and for readings in discussion sections. Like any multipurpose tool, however, a reader may serve none of the possible purposes as well as more specific books. Readers are also somewhat difficult to integrate into the course; the level of knowledge they assume and their points of view may not fit easily into your plans. (Furthermore, adding a large reader to the not inconsiderable text yields a substantial reading load, especially for freshmen.)

If more specific works are to be used, you may select from several reprint series, such as those of Bobbs-Merrill or *Scientific American* (see Section IIC1), you may choose a book on some particular area of interest, you may select one of McCollom's "thrillers" (noted above), or you may suggest readings in either popular or professional literature. Each of these choices has merit for particular functions.

You must decide what will best serve the functions you have chosen for the course and still be manageable. If you use separate readings for discussion sections, for example, you will have to order well in advance and may run into supply problems if a number of different books are ordered from different publishers. (*Teaching of Psychology* offers numerous suggestions of other instructors for supplementary readings.)

8. Term Papers. Instructors sometimes choose to supplement course reading by assigning term papers, either on specified topics or on some topic of the students' choosing. Reading for such papers varies with the type of paper expected. There are three kinds of term papers usually favored for introductory courses:

a. Research papers, which require students to read and synthesize several original research articles. For example, if the topic were brainwashing, suggested reading might include one article on techniques of persuasion, another on sensory deprivation, and another on group pressure. The students' task would be to integrate ideas from each of these articles into a meaningful whole.

b. Small-scale research projects, which students design in order to answer some question in psychology or to demonstrate a known principle. Students may also be asked to carry out small studies of their own, such as a simple experiment in verbal conditioning. Reading would consist of one or two articles on the topic of the experiment.

c. Analysis of a personal experience, observation, or enthusiasm, which students would be expected to interpret in terms of the psychological principles they had learned in the course. (Although this method usually produces great variability among student papers, it is a good way of demonstrating the application of psychology on a personal level.)

When assigning term papers, you may wish to allow students to choose topics and then help them find appropriate readings. While this can work for a small class, it is almost inevitable that your introductory psychology class will be too large for this to be practical. It is probably more practical to list several possible topics with relevant readings for each. Leaving term papers entirely up to student ingenuity is not recommended. Most beginning students are not sufficiently familiar with psychological theory and methodology to make their efforts worthwhile. You can help by choosing the topics and readings. (A useful reference for them, as well as for your more advanced students, is R. J. Sternberg's *Writing the Psychology Paper.* Barron's Educational Series, Inc., 1977.)

A second problem is the temptation for students to plagiarize. While this problem can never be eliminated, the assignment of particular topics minimizes the ready availability of complete papers for the students to duplicate. Requiring several short papers is also probably preferable, since students are less likely to pad them with extensive quotations.

Only instructors with relatively small classes (unusual in introductory psychology) or those with grading assistance may be able to afford term papers at all because of the difficulty of reading and grading large numbers of them. One way of overcoming this is to keep them short, as suggested earlier, and to grade them simply, perhaps only pass/fail. Another way is to use them for only some students. Contract systems of course organization, for example (as discussed in Section IIB10), may require term papers only for students working for an A.

Despite all of these difficulties, term papers can be rewarding experiences for introductory psychology students. The materials covered and ideas explored are likely to be remembered long after other facts learned in the course are forgotten.

9. Sections, Labs, and Teaching Assistants (TAs). Obviously the first decision here is whether you will have sections or labs. If you are to have any form of section or laboratory, then you will need TAs and will have to make numerous further decisions. (If you, the reader, are a TA, many of these decisions may very well be yours; some almost certainly will be.)

For most instructors, the decision to have sections of any kind or not will probably be based on school precedent and already determined. If you are to have them, fine; you need now to consider how to do it. If you cannot have sections, perhaps you might as well skip this discussion. If you are undecided, however (as in the development of a new course), you might consider ways of creating them for the course.

One way of dealing with laboratory or discussion sections is to set them up as a separate course, probably for some fraction of the weight given to a conventional course, to allow the addition of new material without the deletion of a similar amount of other material. Also, by assigning to the main course and the sections appropriate fractions of the total course credit previously given, these sections can be separated from a course in which they had been an integral component.

Sections can then be optional, to be taken only in conjunction with the main course, but not required (or required only of some students—for example, potential psychology majors). Making the sections optional in this way has several benefits. It allows a closer fit to student interests and needs, and it permits the management of the sections or labs with fewer TAs, less room space, and so on.

In deciding what kinds of sections to use, what their content will be, and especially if you wish to attempt to institute sections where there have been none before, you need to consider their advantages and disadvantages. Topic-discussion sections serve a function that the typical large introductory course cannot otherwise serve. They meet in smaller classes where discussion is more feasible, both to develop a sense of participation and to actively engage conceptual thought. Other potential benefits include modeling effects from the TAs, the element of choice itself, and the possibility of students spending more time on a subtopic of interest to them. (For a more detailed consideration of the potential benefits and implementation of topic-discussion sections, see Section IIIC.)

Types of sections other than topic-discussion may offer different advantages. Review and general discussion sections allow more drill, as well as more feedback and interaction, and thus may be advantageous for a more thorough grounding in the basic material. Laboratories can allow the demonstration of psychology as a science, help develop logical and analytic thought processes in the students, and make at least some of the concepts covered in the course more concrete.

Lest you become too enamored—and later disillusioned—however, consider some of the disadvantages of sections. Instituting sections to replace one lecture a week, for example, is almost certain to *cost* you time and effort, not save it. Recruiting, training, and meeting with your TAs, as well as organizing the many necessary details, can be much more time consuming than planning and delivering the lectures. Furthermore, as you become experienced the effort involved does not diminish as much as it does with lecturing.

Until you are confronted with them, you may not appreciate the magnitude of the organizational tasks alone, especially at a large school. It seems that whatever the degree of organization with which you approach these tasks, problems crop up. Exactly how are students to be split up into sections? How are topics to be chosen? Are readings to be used and if so, what? If numerous different readings are used, can you choose and order them early enough to ensure delivery? What do you do when, even so, something does not arrive? (Section IIIC3 considers these issues in more detail.)

Laboratory sections have their own special problems. It is typically more difficult to delegate authority for them to TAs because of equipment problems, potential student injuries, and possibly even insurance requirements. Having them at all obviously requires more specialized facilities and equipment than having discussion sections. In considering the use of laboratories, you may wish to read the appropriate sections of the publications listed at the end of Section I. The APA's Red Book, for example, reviews 22 laboratory manuals and provides lists of equipment and animal suppliers (excerpted in Section IIC6); the Gray Book discusses the issues involved in a laboratory-oriented course.

The TA is a crucial factor in all section decisions. Depending on the system used, TAs may be graduate or undergraduate students; if undergraduate, they may be upperclass psychology majors or students who took the course only the preceding semester. They may be volunteers, interested primarily in obtaining teaching experience, or they may be "coerced volunteers," fulfilling a school requirement or working only for the salary offered. They may be experienced veterans of a dozen or more previous sections or totally inexperienced. They may be students already well known to the instructor, or they may be strangers. It is likely, however, that they will be a mixture of all of these.

Ideal TAs will be responsible, enthusiastic volunteers knowledgeable in their chosen subjects. Of these desired characteristics, maximum knowledge of psychology is probably *not* one of the most important characteristics, and this is itself not necessarily defined by graduate versus undergraduate status. (Several papers concerned specifically with the use of undergraduate TAs, including their selection and their functions in topic-discussion groups and in a "mastery" plan, are presented in the March 1973 newsletter of the APA's Division Two; see Section IIC2 for details. See also "Improving Undergraduate Lecture Classes by Use of Student-Led Discussion Groups," *American Psychologist* 37 (1972): 978.)

One potential problem with sections concerns possible disadvantages for the TAs themselves. If all goes well, sections may be gratifying for both TAs and students, both of them learning and growing from the experience. On the other hand, the TAs can all too easily wind up feeling disillusioned, bitter, hostile, apathetic, and so on, based on such factors as how voluntary their TA participation is and whether they have been allowed to choose their own topic, as well as such unpredictables as interactions in the section meeting or unrealistic teaching ideals. If—or more likely when—this occurs, it is of course also a bad experience for the students. Helping TAs to realistically confront their tasks is thus an important function for the instructor, for the sake of both the TAs and the students in the introductory course. Both TAs and instructor need to recognize that the TAs will face problems new to them and will need help; the TAs have to be willing to bring up their problems and the instructor needs to encourage them to do so and to listen and help when they do.

Overall, while sections have potential problems, they can be very advantageous. Thus, in choosing to use them, as well as in the mechanics of doing so, decide why you are choosing them, what form(s) will best serve your purposes, how you can integrate them with the other elements of the course, and how you can best plan to minimize the potential problems. (See Section IIIC for further detailed suggestions.)

10. Evaluation of Student Performance. For the most part, "evaluation of student performance" will in practical terms mean "grading," which for a large introductory psychology course will often translate as "testing." But it is useful at the outset to remember the various reasons for grading and for testing so that decisions regarding them may be informed and considered rather than automatic.

Evaluation of student performance theoretically serves the feedback needs of students, instructors, and the school. It enables students to judge the results of their study and to modify study habits as necessary, instructors to judge the efficacy of their teaching, and the school to make judgments about students and/or instructors. Of these, the feedback to students is typically given the most emphasis.

In addition, however, final course grades become a part of students' permanent records and may later be used with other criteria in determining their admission into graduate schools and/or jobs, thus, to some extent, influencing their whole careers. Because of the lifetime importance of this latter function it is often the tail that wags the dog. Both the behavior of your students in seeking that ever-higher GPA and your behavior in giving grades will be strongly influenced by this function of evaluation and it may easily override the previously noted uses. If it were a question, for most students, of knowing how they really stand or of getting a good final grade, there is little doubt of their choice.

It seems that the only reasonable solution is to recognize this problem and attempt to live with it, trying to be as fair to all of the students as possible and yet still trying to serve as many evaluative subfunctions as can be feasibly worked in. For most introductory psychology courses, where competitive grading is applied to a large class, this will typically mean grading on a "curve," as is discussed below.

One particular way to avoid the usual competitive grading, however, is to use "mastery" or "contract" systems. Such systems have received a good deal of attention in recent years and have acquired both supporters and critics. The general idea of mastery systems is that an introductory course should provide a specified minimum level of competence for all students. Such plans then test not one student versus another, but each student's achievement of basic competence.

Typically, mastery systems provide a series of tests, with several alternate forms, for each text chapter or a segment of the course. Students are expected to pass each test at a specified level of success but may retake the same test or an alternate form several times to reach this level. The goal is to design the tests so that, with appropriate effort, virtually all students can achieve some stated minimal mastery of the material.

The best known of the formal mastery systems is the "Keller plan," named for its originator, F. S. Keller. Since Keller published the now frequently noted paper "Good-bye Teacher" in 1968 (listed, together with several others, at the end of this discussion) hundreds of college psychology courses have used the system, and it is likely to be of more importance in the future. The general outlines of the Keller plan are noted below, but this handbook cannot provide a comprehensive discussion. (Such a discussion is provided by the Kulik and others paper, which summarizes the growing literature on the Keller plan in science teaching, much of it in introductory psychology. Ryan has also summarized the applications of the plan, but the most recent and most comprehensive of the references shown below is that of Johnson and Ruskin. Chapters in that work summarize the Keller plan, or

Personalized System of Instruction (PSI), plus other behavioral plans, and analyze and compare these; each chapter has an extensive bibliography. If you are considering such a plan, this offering of APA's would be your best first step.)

A PSI plan in its complete form has five features that distinguish it from conventional teaching procedures, all of them details of the primary mastery notion: (1) the basic information for the course is presented in a series of printed study guides, one per unit of the course (where in the simplest form a unit is the equivalent of a text chapter); (2) students demonstrate "mastery" of the course by passing an exam on each unit; (3) the mastery exams are administered by undergraduate "tutors," usually selected from those who did well in the course the preceding term; (4) the pacing of each student's progress is self-determined (and more than one term may be required for completion); (5) a few lectures are given, but they are designed to be stimulating and motivating and may even be used as "rewards" for those who complete course units on time. Note that the result is really a different total *system of instruction*, one in which more than the evaluative function differs from conventional systems.

If you wish to consider a PSI plan, or some variation, see the discussion and references below. Note, however, that the existing supplements for *Introduction to Psychology* can be used to develop such a course. *The Mastery Study Guide* and *Mastery Instructor's Guide*, described in Section IVC, provide the necessary components for points 1 and 2. For suggestions on the use of the undergraduate tutors (point 3), see the article on such use in the APA Division Two Newsletter of March 1973. (See Section IIC2 for details of APA offerings.) For the occasional stimulating lectures (point 5) see the suggestions in Section VI; a number of these include demonstrations or lecture topics that expand on text material.

Results for the Keller plan (as summarized by Kulik and others) show it to be invariably attractive to students, with the self-pacing and personal interaction with tutors and instructor the features most favored. In addition, students report that they both learn more and work harder for such courses. (Both reports are supported by some objective data.) The major disadvantage noted in the Kulik paper has been the high withdrawal rate found in some cases. This is by no means true for all cases, however; some courses have even had lower rates of withdrawal than conventional courses. Kulik and others report that observed high rates of withdrawal seem to result from procrastination and that systems for discouraging procrastination being developed by numerous users seem to have been instrumental in lowering withdrawal rates.

It is also possible to set up a "contract" system, which may or may not include elements of a mastery system. The basic notion of a contract system is that each student may choose, at the beginning of the course, whether to seek an A, B, or C grade, the achievement of each being based on specifiable performances. In a course using mastery elements, for example, a C might be equivalent to a grade of 70 percent or better on each unit, with perhaps no further work necessary. An A or B might then require higher scores on each unit—maybe 90 percent and 80 percent, respectively. Additional work might also be required, such as a term paper for an A. Such a system allows students to decide in advance what level of work they wish to perform and sets clear standards for that work, independent of how many other students elect to work that hard or harder. Thus, it has advantages of clear standards, student choice and behavioral commitment, lack of directly competitive pressures for a fixed number of As, and so on.

Mastery and contract forms of noncompetitive evaluation share several disadvantages: Both require a substantial extra effort in planning and test writing before the course is taught and in test giving and other evaluative procedures while it is under way. In addition, both have their own problems.

One major problem with the mastery system is the students who pass segments at the required level—for example, 70 percent—but do so at a slow rate and so complete only part of the material. Whereas these students might otherwise have had only a *partial* understanding of *all* the course, here they would have a *solid* basic understanding of only *part* of the course. Keller would allow them to continue work in the following term. But do they then take an overload or not take some other course? What if another course they wish to take lists introductory psychology as a prerequisite? Any time you make such a major change in course format you must expect a new range of such problems.

In the contract system, a major problem is whether the contracting for a given grade ensures that the students get that grade under any circumstances, only if a substantial effort has been made, or only if the students in fact meet some stated level of achievement. This is more complicated than it may seem. Some instructors, for example, believe that students who contract to do the work for an A should get the A; they feel that if the students don't complete the requirements it will be on their conscience and will motivate them in the future. Others feel that the contract must be completed if it is to be termed a "contract."

Another problem is that absolute standards have to be set before it is known what percentage of students will achieve them, or even if any students can. This risks penalizing last year's students by giving an inordinate number of As or penalizing current students by making an A too difficult to achieve. What tends to happen, if the instructor is attempting to strike a fair balance, is that the standards must be revised during the teaching of the course. This simultaneously adds to the already substantial problems of administering the course and reduces some of the value of the system in that the "set" standards for achievement are, in fact, changed.

Thus, in deciding to use any variation of such plans a whole new set of decisions arises. More detail on these plans is beyond the scope of this handbook; those interested are referred to the sources below, especially the Johnson and Ruskin

22

summary. For continuing help, you should get on the mailing list of the Center for Personalized Instruction; several of their publications are noted below, but they also sponsor national conferences on personalized education (the fifth one in 1979) and offer a variety of books, papers, and audiovisual aids, as well as the *PSI Newsletter.* Their address is 29 Loyola Hall, Georgetown University, Washington, D.C., 20057.

Fraley, L. E., and Vargas, E. A. (eds.) (1976) *Behavioral Research and Technology in Higher Education.* Gainesville, Fla.: University of Florida.

Johnson, K. R., and Ruskin, R. S. (1977) *Behavioral Instruction: An Evaluative Review.* Washington, D.C.: APA.

Johnston, J. M. (ed.) (1975) *Behavior Research and Technology in Higher Education.* Springfield, Ill.: Charles C. Thomas.

Keller, F. S. (1968) Good-bye Teacher. *Journal of Applied Behavior Analysis,* 1:78–89.

Keller, F. S. (1974) Ten Years of Personalized Instruction. *Teaching of Psychology,* 1:1–8.

Kulik, J. A., Kulik, C. L., and Carmichael, K. (1974) The Keller Plan in Science Teaching. *Science,* 183:379–83.

PSI Newsletter, Washington, D.C.: Center for Personalized Instruction, Georgetown University.

Ruskin, R. S. (1974) *Individualized Instruction in Higher Education: A Bibliography.* Washington, D.C.: Center for Personalized Instruction, Georgetown University.

Ryan, B. A. (1974) *Keller's Personalized System of Instruction: An Appraisal.* Washington, D.C.: APA.

Sherman, J. G., and Lazar, R. (eds.) (1977) *Personalized Instruction in Higher Education: Proceedings of the Third National Conference.* Washington, D.C.: Center for Personalized Instruction, Georgetown University.

If you do not choose a mastery or contract system as described above, you can either go directly to some form of competitive or curve grading or attempt an intermediate form. Such an intermediate form might use conventional testing, for example, but set fixed standards for As and Bs so that students do not directly compete against each other and one student's A does not necessarily force another's B.

The problem with such an intermediate form is that it hides an *implicit* curve, and in hiding it runs greater risks of being unfair to the students. A curve is implicit in that you must already know how much an A student can be expected to achieve in order to be able to set the "preset" standards of accomplishment; the risks derive from this estimate of standards. If your standards are too demanding, as they will be if you set levels based on previous teaching experience with a more highly selected student population, very few students will get As. The extreme form of this problem is noted in an anecdote reported by Walker and McKeachie, in which a distinguished visiting researcher at a major midwestern university drew all of the prize graduate students by his reputation, then "failed" virtually all of them by assigning "one C, five or 6 Ds, and over 20 Es," based on his own unrealistic standards of achievement (Walker and McKeachie, listed at the end of Section I).

On the other hand, if your standards are too low, you risk giving too many As. While this initially seems less of a problem—certainly the students receiving them will not object—it nevertheless is unfair to *other* students. It reduces the value of an A for those students who have taken the course in previous semesters, and it dilutes the value of the A for the top students in the current course by failing to differentiate them from a large group of less capable or less well prepared students.

It seems, then, that there is no way of avoiding competitive grading if you are to be fair to all students. This is a result *not* of any necessity for information feedback to student, instructor, or school, but of the competitive pressure applied from *outside* the school—that is, by graduate schools or prospective employers. So long as there are more applicants than positions, and so long as specific class grades and GPAs are used as selection criteria for these positions, the best advice for an instructor would seem to be grin and bear it.

Virtually any attempt by an instructor to personally "beat" such a system only cheats or hinders some students at the expense of others. Even the elimination of grades does not really help. If it is done sporadically, as in some schools' pass/fail systems, a "pass" is likely to be considered by the outside agencies as the equivalent of a C or C−. If an entire school drops grades, students from that school who wish to compete for graduate school or jobs are simply rated on other criteria, often, as with graduate record exams, criteria with greater possible sources of bias and error than GPAs—if they are not, in fact, dropped from the competition entirely.

If the competitive grade bind is truly as described, and the author of this handbook believes that it is, what can you do to be fair to as many students as possible? The answer seems to lie in a careful use of that old student bugaboo, the grading curve. The type of curve suggested is one in which similar, though not necessarily identical, percentages of the class receive As, Bs, and Cs from one term to the next. Introductory psychology is typically taken by a major percentage of a school's student body, and in large enough numbers that the members of a given class can be considered close to a random sample of all the students who will be taking the course. The use of set percentages of As and Bs assumes both that you have about the same students one time as another and that they work about as hard. While these assumptions might not be exactly true, they are better than other possible ones. By using only approximately set percentages, you can adjust somewhat each time, to set the dividing lines at gaps in the histogram or, as you gain more experience over several classes, even to adjust for a perceived difference in overall student performance. (Note that as you begin doing the latter, you are in effect building an implicit curve based on several terms' experience.

A grading curve need not be perfectly normal in shape since testing patterns will affect the shape, and it need not yield any particular numbers of As, Bs, and Cs. It *should*, however, be based on total points achieved, with Z-score transformations used if the exams or other grade components are not similarly distributed. And it is wise to set the grade lines for individual exams a bit more severely than you intend to in the long run. This allows you to resolve marginal cases upward in the final grades, a procedure that both you and the students will find desirable. While there are other possible variations in details, using a set of total scores to rank all students, and choosing even approximate percentages for A, B, and C constitute a curve form of grading. In making the many further decisions about testing and grading that are required, this concept of curve grading will often be relevant, although sometimes only implicit.

What, then, are these other decisions? First of all, the relative importance of the various components already chosen for the course needs to be stated in terms of grading. If sections are used, what percentage of the grade are they to represent? Or are they to be separately graded in some way—for example, optional sections given separate credit? Are there written inputs such as lab reports or papers, turned in via sections or directly to the instructor? Are special projects of any sort required or encouraged?

In all cases, these must be considered in terms of the grading to be done as well as their educational relevance. In fact, sometimes the two factors may be in opposition; the pressure of grading may bias the students' behavior in a way that will reduce the educational benefits. If this seems to be true for a particular component of your course, you may wish to minimize the grading on that component. Some grading value may have to be retained, however, to provide enough extrinsic motivation to ensure completion of the assignment.

The practical problems of grading large numbers of students, however, will typically dictate that papers, projects, and so on, will probably not form much of the grades, and those that do will probably do so via the sections, being graded by the TAs. The primary problems of evaluation, especially for the new instructor, will thus reduce to those of testing itself, and primarily objective testing. (Section IIIC7 considers in detail some of the issues involved in grading discussion sections.)

The issue of whether or not *only* objective testing is used pits motivational and study-habit factors against grading problems. Students often (rightly or wrongly) feel that they know more than is measured by an objective test or that they can answer essay questions better than objective ones. In addition, it seems apparent that study habits encouraged by all-objective testing will be different than they would be if essay questions were also used. To the extent that such a difference means concentrating on detail to the detriment of larger issues, we can all agree that this is not desirable.

On the other hand, the further you move away from fixed-answer objective questions, the harder grading becomes. Fill-in-the-blanks, or finish-the-sentence, or identify-the-following are subject to more student interpretation and instructor grading problems and take more time to score than multiple-choice. And if TAs or outside graders help in the grading, more care must be taken to obtain reliability across graders. If a number of short essays are used, or fewer longer ones, these problems mount. For any essay question, reliable grading virtually requires that all answers to that question be graded by one person and that all essays be read through before they are graded. If the number of students is in the hundreds, as is often the case for introductory psychology, only a few brief essay questions are even marginally feasible and those at the cost of substantial grading effort. Even then, the grading reliability is open to serious question.

Thus, the students get the chance to write a few essay questions in exchange for a massive increase in grading effort of somewhat dubious reliability. Since only a few such questions can be asked, and these should be relatively constrained to improve grader reliability, there is also the question of validity—the extent to which these few questions reflect students' knowledge of the wide range of topics typically included in even the fraction of the course covered by one exam. In contrast, using a number of short objective questions allows more of these topics to be tested in a single exam. This both encourages students to complete all of the reading and is more likely to fairly represent students' relative capabilities. In general, "objective" (for example, multiple-choice) tests are the hardest to write but the easiest to grade; in contrast, the broad general essay exam is the easiest to write but the hardest to grade.

Despite the grading problems with broad general questions, however, it is nonetheless true that students who expect to be asked such questions are thereby encouraged to study in a probably advantageous manner, a benefit not to be lightly dismissed. One way of obtaining this advantage without excessive penalties is to include essay questions but minimize the grading problems, either by reducing the grading importance of these questions or by reducing the range of possible grades applied to them. The ultimate step in this direction is not to grade them at all. This latter method has, in fact, been used by highly reputable instructors in order to encourage desired study habits. It does seem, however, to offer potential problems in instructor-student relations, especially so the more the instructor attempts to make grading practices specified and public, as is suggested below.

Feasibility of grading is not the only argument in support of at least primarily objective testing. Another is the fact that an introductory course typically puts more emphasis on learning a broad range of basic information and less on conceptual thinking than do more advanced courses. This course orientation is naturally suited to objective testing.

Note that this is *not* saying that either introductory psychology *or* objective testing is limited solely to memorization functions. Learning to use concepts is clearly a part of the course and can be tested via multiple-choice questions if they are carefully written and selected. Such questions are provided separately, in the Test Item File, described in detail in Section IVD. These questions have been written to test concepts as well as mere rote memorization. (Suggestions for building exams are included in Section IVD3 and suggestions for essay questions are included in Section VI. See Section IVC for details of ready-made exams available in the *Mastery Instructor's Guide.*)

In addition to the type of testing to be used, of course, you must decide what components will be included: clearly, the *Introduction to Psychology* readings and probably any required supplementary readings will be, but what of other course elements? Are lectures to be included, for example, or special demonstrations, or perhaps films? You must make your own choices, based on your own personal philosophy, your school's practices, and your students' responses. If lectures are to be tested, for example, this has the advantage of increasing attendance, but also yields extensive note taking—often, though not necessarily, to the detriment of understanding. Remember the old and trite, but perhaps true, statement: "The lecture system is a way of transferring information from the instructor's notes to the student's notes without it passing through the heads of either." If your lectures cover material not in the text, perhaps you should consider lecture passouts (as noted in Section IIIA3) and test on the passout material. If they mostly repeat the text, perhaps using only text-based testing is adequate. You must decide.

There are, however, yet other decisions you will face regarding testing. You might as well consider them now, since they will be almost certain to arise later. Several of them center about the problems of make-up exams. Because of the large size of the typical course, the odds are great that some students will be indisposed (for example, in the infirmary) for any particular exam. Do you allow them to take the same exam later? Do you make up an alternate? If you do the former, you run the risk of cheating; if you do the latter, you double your work and then remain unsure of the grade equivalent since the alternate exam will have no "normative" data to ensure its comparability to the regular one.

In addition to the obviously indisposed, there will be other students less obviously so: the "I was sick and stayed home" students, and others with similarly questionable excuses. You may even have a third category, especially likely if your school permits freshmen to take the course: the "I was scared (or not prepared) and stayed home" students. You may or may not let students of either of these categories take the same exam or an alternate for partial or full credit. But it will help you in dealing with such problems if you have already devised a contingency plan.

You may also wish to consider another type of make-up exam. In some schools students who do especially badly on an exam are allowed to retake the same exam later. Since this is obviously not comparable to a regular exam, there is a limit as to how much this can help their grade: the final grade might be limited to C if based on any such retake exams, for example. Such a procedure might seem strange, but consider this: Studying for and retaking the same exam does help the students at the bottom of the curve to learn the material. (In that sense it is like the mastery system selectively applied.) And, after all, is not the students' learning the material what we really want? The extra administrative effort involved and the giving of a few Cs rather than Ds or Fs may not be a bad price to pay for increased student effort and knowledge.

Although it is not likely to confront many instructors, a few will have to decide about special exam-taking procedures. Some of these will come to you—for example, blind students, who must have exams read aloud and must dictate answers. Others may never be seen unless you look for them—for example, students whose command of English is so limited that their effective time for doing the exam is reduced substantially by the time taken to read it; or students operating under transient situational distress, such as a death in the family, who will take the exam, but do poorly. You may want to know about such problems and to provide special arrangements accordingly.

As in other decision areas, your handling of these make-up problems or special arrangements will necessarily reflect both your own opinions and your school's norms. The best approach is probably to try to decide ahead of the actual event what you will do, perhaps aided by the advice of someone else in your department. You may even wish to tell the students your rules as part of the course introduction, assuming that you have them worked out; it might save both them and you some later problems.

You should keep in mind, however, that no student is likely to obtain a zero score on an exam. (It is clearly impossible on a multiple-choice exam.) Thus, whether or not you give make-up exams for full credit, the giving of "zero" marks for missed exams is both morally and statistically unjustified. Such marks are specifically punitive and have no relationship to level of achievement in the course. (If you *intend* to be punitive, there are probably fairer ways.)

Another decision you must face concerns the antagonistic goals of maximum student feedback, on the one hand, and security of your exam questions, on the other. It will be much easier if you can work on building one or a few good versions of each exam you use rather than writing a completely new one each time. Furthermore, even the number of questions provided in the Test Item File may become limiting if you try to build several new exams each semester. Yet the only way that you can use only one or two exams without future students attempting to memorize the questions—or worse, just the answers—is to prevent the distribution of the

28

exams. Instructors thus often collect the questions at the end of the exam—perhaps going so far as to count or even number them, to ensure the return of all copies. But this deprives the students of informational feedback, which we psychologists tell them is useful in maximizing learning.

One way of partially alleviating this problem is to allow the students later controlled access to the exam: by spending a class meeting on the exam and again collecting all copies, or by providing a supervised location where interested students can examine a copy. If you do the latter, incidentally, students find it very helpful if the copy is annotated with not only the correct answer but also the source—for example, text page number. (Both are, of course, included for each question in the Test Item File.)

If you decide to withhold exams as a rule, you may also wish to provide a simple, short "sample" exam that new students *can* look at, or even test themselves with, in lieu of studying your old exams. This helps relieve fear of the unknown and provides them some insight into your testing philosophy. If you do this, be sure to make the sample *realistic*, to avoid unnecessary panic or misleading expectations. (Self-quizzes in the *Study Guide* and *Mastery Study Guide* can also serve this purpose.)

A related exam-security question concerns proctoring or monitoring of the exam itself. You will need to strike some intermediate point between an authoritarian jailer approach and one so lax that cheating is encouraged; no one likes the former, while the latter is undesirable for many reasons, not the least being that if curve grading is used it will reward cheaters at the expense of honest students.

A further problem with attempting to control all exams is that if a few do get out, they provide their possessors with an unfair advantage. Especially where organized systems exist to encourage such activity—for example, some fraternities and sororities—students may be able to get copies of your exams despite your precautions. Obviously this is easier for a few essay questions that can be temporarily memorized, but it may happen even with multiple-choice exams. If this is the case and you give the same exam, you have just cooperated in a system of rewarding cheating and punishing honesty—albeit unknowingly.

If you suspect such problems, one advisable technique is to use several alternate forms of each exam, with questions or pages rearranged. The use of several such forms for the same exam helps cut down cheating on that exam, while the use of them from one term to another helps minimize cheating based on a list of answers versus question numbers. (It doesn't cut cheating based on memorizing the questions, but at least those students have learned *something*.)

In the absence of firm personal convictions on such matters, it is probably wise to utilize whatever system has been used at your school before. But *plan* to do something; don't wait until you begin to run out of questions before deciding to hold on to your exams, or until cheating is rampant before proctoring.

The central reason for going to this length in discussing testing should also be kept firmly in mind: Testing is an emotionally charged problem area, fraught with issues that help no one and often distress all participants. In a course in which the first exam occurs in midterm, this is the time when you tend to become "the enemy," and half a semester's carefully cultivated rapport can evaporate, leaving sullen hostility. For this reason, as well as others, some instructors give exams more often, perhaps every two weeks. This is more testing effort, for the instructor and the students, and of course absorbs class time, but it has several advantages. In addition to simply providing practice at taking this kind of exam, it allows the course to be absorbed in more manageable chunks, it reduces the importance of any particular exam, and it provides both students and instructor with information about students' trends. (Note that testing in this way is similar to some aspects of a mastery system, as described earlier.)

Remember that from your point of view the tests may be simple measuring devices, to be made as accurate and precise as possible, but mostly to be gotten out of the way so as to get on with the real elements of the course. To the students, however, they may be *the* events of the course, coloring their entire perspective of both you and psychology. If you recognize this and work to overcome the inherent problems, you can minimize them. If you ignore this, you do so at your peril, risking not only student emnity but possible costs in such tangibles as salary and tenure, which are becoming increasingly sensitive to student input. (Note Section VA.)

The key to minimizing test problems, which should be kept in mind in making various decisions previously noted, is to *plan what you are doing and why.* Make decisions based on fairness to students insofar as possible, be responsive to student distress, offer whatever aids to study and testing you can, and be sure that they know what you are doing. Students should probably have *full* information on how your tests are constructed, scored, and graded, for example. This won't make the problems go away, but if you're lucky it will allow you—and the students—to live with them.

In the author's view, the grading-testing situation is one into which both students and instructor are locked by outside pressures and linked together. If both attempt to understand their relationship and to make it mutually supportive, it can be symbiotic—life-giving for each. If both seek to best the other, however, it can be more akin to a suicide pact.

For further discussion of testing and grading problems, see the McKeachie and Walker and McKeachie references at the end of Section I and the references listed below. In addition, Singer's JSAS bibliography (noted in Section IIC2) gives other references for grading and *Teaching of Psychology* often includes articles on related topics.

Kirschenbaum, H., and others (1971) *Wa Ja Get?* New York: Hart.

Lamberth, J. (1975) To Curve or Not to Curve: The Defense. *Teaching of Psychology*, 2:82–83.

Sax, G. (1974) *Principles of Educational Measurement and Evaluation.* Belmont, Calif.: Wadsworth Publishing.

Scheirer, C. J. (1975) To Curve or Not to Curve: The Complaint. *Teaching of Psychology*, 2:82.

Thorndike, R. L. (ed.) (1971) *Educational Measurement.* Washington, D.C.: American Council on Education.

11. Student Evaluation of the Course and Instructor. Section V presents details of the purposes and possible systems for student evaluations of you and your course. This section is limited to a consideration of your decisions regarding the use of such evaluation systems. Before *making* these decisions you should also read Section V. (See also the APA's Gray Book.)

Clearly, your primary decision is whether you will, in fact, use any such evaluation system. For some of you, that decision will already have been made; the use of mandatory evaluation systems seems to be increasing. For others of you, the systems will be available and suggested, but the use optional. For still others, the decision to use a system may require developing your own form.

If it is not required, however, why even consider it? Section VB3 points out that from your view, evaluations are more likely to be punishing than rewarding. This may leave you feeling that evaluation is the last thing you want. True, it can be distressing, especially for a new instructor; negative evaluations can be *very* punishing, even when they clearly represent the discontented fringe of a generally satisfied group. (Remember that any volunteer evaluation will yield a biased sample: The dissatisfied are more likely to respond.) The key term is "feedback." If you sincerely wish to improve your teaching, you need feedback. And while some is available from other channels, a comprehensive formal evaluation system provides both qualitative and quantitative information not easily obtained in other ways.

Suppose that you are convinced that evaluation is a good idea. Then what? You need to choose a system: how many forms, covering what aspects of the class, forced-choice or open-end, given at the end or at several times during the course, whether to include a discussion section for live and personal feedback, and so on. Any system that you do choose will then probably be maximally effective if integrated into your class plans and made public knowledge for the students.

Announcing your intent to take feedback can also help students to understand that you are trying to do a good job and can help to get them involved with improving the course. This can help both you and your teaching, not only by telling you what you are doing right (or wrong) but also by suggesting what else to do. Thus, the feedback system can become an aid to mutual support of students and instructor, that is, to the "symbiosis" noted earlier.

C. RESOURCES AVAILABLE TO YOU

1. From Publishers. The supplements specifically designed for *Introduction to Psychology*, Seventh Edition and available from its publisher, Harcourt Brace Jovanovich, Inc., are described in Section IV. But other publishers can also help, primarily through the way in which education-oriented publications are merchandised. (Those of you who are familiar with book sales representatives, catalogs, and free desk copies may skip the following, but for the neophyte instructor, it may be eye opening.)

Assuming that those of you now reading are new to such things, it is likely that you have until now purchased most of your own books. No more need this be the case. While certain works not intended for class use are not available, a striking collection of books *is* available to you for the asking. Books used in classrooms are typically not advertised in the manner of toothpaste, and so on. Instead the advertising budget is expended in attempts to get copies of the books into the hands of those who can control their sales via adoption for courses—that is, you. This is done in several ways. Some publishers send sales representatives to track you down; others rely more on catalogs sent to all listed instructors. In any case, nearly all are responsive to direct requests from you for a desk or examination copy of a book you might reasonably use for a course.

This system admirably serves the needs of all concerned, as long as it is not abused, and you are strongly encouraged to include it in your planning. Section IIB7, for example, lists several ways that supplementary readings might be used with the introductory course. If you wish to consider any or all of them, spending your own money is *not* the way to do it. If you know of a book that you might be interested in, drop a note to the publisher asking for a copy. If you are in a hurry, see if there is a local office or sales representative. Write on departmental letterhead, identify yourself, and state your duties and how the book might be expected to help you. If phoning, do the same and follow up with a letter.

When you are contacted by sales representatives, remember that they are *not* there to *sell* you something, but to *give* you something in hopes that you will help them sell it to your students. These company representatives are often rated by their own company not only on how many instructors they contact, but on how many books they can convince those instructors to take. Don't consider this a license for excessive indulgence; "one of everything" is not the ideal policy. Request copies of books for which you have a reasonably legitimate purpose; sometimes the representatives themselves are able to suggest books that you might not have thought of.

You will find that some publishers won't send free desk copies (and if you ignore the advice in the previous paragraph about greed, this could become more frequent). But even then they will usually offer a professional discount, and a refund if you do adopt the book for a class.

In most cases, the representatives will get around to you once you are listed by a school as an instructor. Then when you request a book it is sent to you from a central shipping point. But it is possible to speed up the process, a fact that might be helpful in planning your first year's course(s). If a book sounds like a good possibility and time is of the essence, the representative may be able to supply you directly with a copy or to expedite delivery of one to you.

The catalogs used by some companies may also be very helpful. They are often well arranged and indexed so that you can find your area(s) of interest. Some catalogs present such a wide range of options that they are valuable reference works—for example, the *Scientific American* reprint catalogs available from Freeman (listed below). Some of the catalogs offer a limited number of free copies, no questions asked. For more than this, or for other catalogs, write to them on letterhead stationery as suggested above. Your department may even have special forms for this purpose, though an individual letter might get better results in a questionable case. In contacting a large publisher "blind," it is best to try to communicate directly with their college sales representatives; your school bookstore is likely to have their names.

You are probably already familiar with the *Books in Print* and *Paperback Books in Print* catalogs; if not, by all means become so. Both your library and your school bookstore should have copies. Given either a title or an author, you should be able to locate any book now in print; the listing provides you with the publisher, whom you may contact as described earlier. *Books in Print* includes a complete listing of publishers and their addresses, in addition to noting who publishes each book listed. Another useful reference is *The Publishers Trade List Annual*, a collection of publishers' catalogs. These can be more useful than *Books in Print* for checking on special series such as those noted on page 40.

Also note that a different kind of published aid to teaching may be found in miscellaneous books, educational committee reports, and so on. Some of the more outstanding of these aids are those given at the end of Section I and the APA publications described in Section IIC2, especially the Red Book (which includes an address list of publishers likely to have useful offerings).

As noted in Section IIB7, one way of providing supplemental reading is to assign one of several types of readers created for this purpose. The most common type is a set of general readings in psychology drawn from many sources and integrated primarily by the editor's interest in them. Most of these readers are organized into subsections, often comparable to the subsections of a typical introductory course. A more specialized type is that organized around a theme; readings are still taken from many sources, but all are oriented to the theme—for example, fundamental issues, humanistic psychology. One specialty reader is made up entirely of selections from the public press, updated each year; others use only science fiction selections, arranged and introduced to relate them to psychological themes. (See references at the end of this section.) Many such readers exist and new ones are constantly being published; those noted at the end of this section are only a sample. If you wish to use a reader, it should not be difficult to find one to suit a particular purpose. (Note that one function of the journal of the APA's Division Two, *Teaching of Psychology*, is to publish reviews of readers and that the APA's Red Book also includes such reviews. Both are listed in Section IIC2.)

Another type of reader is that drawn from a common source—for example, *Scientific American* or, more recently, *American Scientist.* These readers are essentially collected and arranged sets of reprints. They have the advantage of being of a similar technical level throughout but thereby lack some of the more extreme eclecticism of other collections. If you desire only a few of these readings, or wish to edit your own collection, the same sources also provide individual reprints. In addition, other sources provide only individual reprints; these include reprints from *Science* as well as the multiple-source reprints produced by Bobbs-Merrill. As with other publisher offerings, catalogs and samples of reprints for examination are typically available to instructors on request. If you decide to use some in the class they may be ordered through your local bookstore. (See addresses below.)

Xerox offers a system for producing your own reader called the XIP (for Xerox Individualized Publishing) Readings in Psychology System; W. J. McKeachie serves as the project consultant. Via their duplication technique, Xerox will produce a volume of readings containing only your own selections. You are expected to choose most of them from their catalog of well over a thousand already available and cross-indexed articles, but you may include up to 20 percent "new" material: for example, your own index, appendixes, articles for which Xerox can obtain reproduction rights, or even original manuscripts. (Note that titles offered by other reprint systems may not be available for this purpose.) When you have chosen your selections, Xerox copies, compiles, and binds your volume, using your name and title. The price for a volume varies with its size and with the guaranteed order but can be competitive with other readers, especially for larger classes. Xerox also offers a collection of the best of the XIP volumes created by other instructors, so that in effect Xerox becomes another publisher to consider as a source of books (see Rivenbark and Rosenberg on p. 39). This system is likely to be most appealing to instructors with large classes (because of the economics involved) and to those whose needs are for a specialized reader not currently offered, which they expect to use repeatedly (because of the effort involved in creating it). (For further information, write to Xerox College Publishing, 191 Spring St., Lexington, Mass. 02173.)

Another way to supplement student reading (as noted in Section IIB7) is to use some of the series of short paperback monographs devoted to specific topics. They are particularly useful if you wish students to pursue one or two areas of psychology in depth, since the monographs often provide more coverage than the corresponding chapter in *Introduction to Psychology*, Seventh Edition. However, individual volumes vary greatly in quality and in value to beginning students. Several series are currently available (including those listed at the end of this section); complete information on titles, contents, and prices may be obtained directly from the publishers. For further suggested supplements, see the APA's Red Book, which includes not only reviews of readers noted above, but also notes on periodicals, novels, and popular books, as well as extensive lists of supplementary books arranged by topic.

The final source to be noted here is the comprehensive *Harvard List of Books in Psychology*, 4th ed. (Cambridge, Mass.: Harvard University Press, 1971). This list, updated or recompiled at periodic intervals by a group of Harvard psychologists, is broken down into over 30 categories, from "Reference Works and Basic Handbooks" to "Psychic Research and Parapsychology."

The readings listed below are by no means comprehensive but represent good recent examples of the type of materials available and should provide you with an adequate set of options until you can develop your own sources more fully. All are paperbacks, and typically retail for about four to six dollars though a few are also available in hardbound editions (see *Books in Print*). Most are approximately 6" by 9", but some, as noted in the descriptions are 8½" by 11". Virtually all are arranged in sections intended to reflect the usual portions of the classic introductory psychology course.

READERS

Atkinson, R. C. (ed.) (1975) *Psychology in Progress: Readings from Scientific American.* San Francisco: W. H. Freeman, 392 pp. (8½ x 11 format). Thirty-nine selections, all from *Scientific American*, originally published from 1951 through 1974. A wide range of topics, numerous well-known authors and articles, and *Scientific American*'s excellent illustrations. An introduction to each subsection, original bibliographies, and an index.

Cohen, I. S. (ed.) (1975) *Perspectives on Psychology: Introductory Readings.* New

York: Praeger, 464 pp. Thirty-five selections of several kinds, ranging from scientific journal articles through behavioral scientists' writings for general readership to essays by nonscientists, the latter including, for example, George Bernard Shaw. Original bibliographies.

Doyle, K. O., Jr. (ed.) (1973) *Interaction: Readings in Human Psychology.* Lexington, Mass.: D. C. Heath, 591 pp. Forty-one contemporary selections intended to be both pedagogically sound and personally interesting to students. Introductions to the book and to each section, original bibliographies, and an index.

Dushkin Publishing Group. (Yearly) *Readings in Psychology.* Guilford, Conn.: Dushkin Publishing Group (8½ x 11 format). A collection of readings (typically about 60) from the popular press (including *American Psychologist*, but more frequently *Time, Playboy, Saturday Review,* and so on) of the several years preceding. Many of them are by the psychologists involved, but others are by staff writers of the publications. Could be very involving for students and certainly could be used to educate them in how to read the popular press, but at the same time it lacks the depth and professionalism found in some other readers. Introductions to each section, a special guide to the articles by topic, an index, and a short list of "runner-up" articles for further reading.

Ekstrand, B. R., and Bourne, L. E., Jr. (eds.) (1974) *Principles and Meanings of Psychology: Readings.* Hinsdale, Ill.: Dryden Press, 511 pp. (8½ x 11 format). Sixty-five recent selections, basically from the technical literature (some of them very well known) but including many from *Time, Newsweek,* and so on.

Estrada, J., and Estrada, E. (eds.) (1977) *The Future of Being Human: Psychology and Science Fiction.* San Francisco: Canfield Press, 173 pp. (8½ x 11 format). Twenty-two science fiction stories chosen "to represent the major areas of psychology and to provide insight into psychological issues." As with the other science fiction readers below, these can be useful to stimulate discussion, but may be of little use as general background in psychology per se. An introduction to the books, study questions for each selection, and a guide to the psychological issues represented in each selection.

Hamsher, J. H., and Sigall, H. (eds.) (1973) *Psychology and Social Issues.* New York: Macmillan, 550 pp. Forty-two selections intended to show students the relevance of psychology in confronting social problems by presenting as role models recent psychologists' efforts that combine a concern for relevance with professional rigor. Organized under topics such as "Environment and Urban Life," "Population Control," and "Race." (Note that while the topics are relevant, the papers are professional; they might consequently be very useful for relatively sophisticated students but could be overwhelming for less advanced students.) Introductions to the book, to each section, and to each paper, plus original bibliographies and an index.

Janis, I. L. (ed.) (1977) *Current Trends in Psychology: Readings from American*

Scientist. Los Altos, Calif.: William Kaufmann, 396 pp. (8½ x 11 format). Thirty-nine selections, all from *American Scientist*, originally published from 1965 through 1977. A wide range of topics, with both the advantages and disadvantages of *American Scientist*: well-known authors and excellent papers, well illustrated and including bibliographies, but typically difficult for students to read, especially at the introductory level. Introductions to the book and to each section, author and subject indexes, and original bibliographies.

Kagan, J., Haith, M. M., and Caldwell, C. (eds.) (1971) *Psychology: Adapted Readings.* New York: Harcourt Brace Jovanovich, 404 pp. Thirty-five selections, both recent and classic, most of them edited to some degree, some of them substantially rewritten. Includes selections not only by Darley and Latané, for example, but also by James, Pavlov, Terman, and so on. An introduction to each section and some bibliographies.

Katz, H. A., Greenberg, M. H., and Warrick, P. S. (eds.) (1977) *Introductory Psychology Through Science Fiction* (2nd ed.). Chicago: Rand McNally, 550 pp. Twenty-eight science fiction selections, with the advantages and disadvantages noted for Estrada and Estrada. An introduction for each section plus a bibliography of psychological readings.

Kimble, D. P. (ed.) (1977) *Contrast and Controversy in Modern Psychology.* Santa Monica, Calif.: Goodyear Publishing, 268 pp. Twenty selections under subsections somewhat different from the usual ones, for example, including "intelligence" but also "the battered child" and "psychosurgery," reflecting the focus of the title. An introduction to the book and original bibliographies.

Kravitz, J., and Hillabrant, W. (eds.) (1977) *The Future Is Now: Readings in Introductory Psychology.* Itasca, Ill.: F. E. Peacock, 446 pp. Sixty selections— all from the popular press, for example, *Psychology Today, Time,* and *Harper's*— considered to be informative, interesting, and of a high level but not pedantic. Introductions to the book and to each section, plus name and subject indexes.

Maas, J. (ed.) (1977) *Readings in Psychology Today* (4th ed.) Westminster, Md.: Random House, 350 pp. (8½ x 11 format). Sixty-five selections from *Psychology Today*, selected for overall interest level on the basis of student evaluations, timeliness, and pedagogical value; of these, 27 are new since the last edition. New section introductions, original bibliographies, and index.

McCauley, C. R., and Stitt, C. L. (eds.) (1976) *Frontiers of Behavior: Perspective and Practice.* New York: Praeger, 231 pp. Eleven selections, covering first the behavioral, cognitive, and ethological perspectives and then issues of applied psychology—for example, television and violence, mental illness—to which these perspectives may be applied. Introductions to the book and to each selection plus original bibliographies.

McCollom, I. N., and Badore, N. L. (eds.) (1973) *Exploring Psychology: Introductory Readings.* New York: Thomas Y. Crowell, 456 pp. Fifty-six selections from many sources, old and new, chosen in support of McCollom's philosophy of such outside reading as "thrillers" ("Psychological Thrillers; Psychology Books Students Read When Given Freedom of Choice." *American Psychologist* 26 (1971): 921–27.) Introduction to the book plus editorial comments before and after each selection to relate them to psychology, to each other, and to the students. Original bibliographies and a glossary.

McKinney, F. (ed.) (1973) *Psychology in Action: Basic Readings* (2nd ed.). New York: Macmillan, 499 pp. Fifty-two selections, from both professional and popular sources, designed to show the student how psychologists use their technology to deal realistically with a variety of immediate problems. Some passages of the professional articles considered too complex have been removed or footnoted and the original bibliographies have been combined into a single bibliography. Each selection has brief suggestions for further reading, introductions, and separately captioned "Implications." Also includes an appendix, "Use of the Selections," and an index.

Melvin, K. B., Brodsky, S. L., and Fowler, R. D., Jr. (eds.) (1977) *Psy-Fi One: An Anthology of Psychology in Science Fiction.* New York: Random House, 301 pp. Twenty science fiction selections, with the advantages and disadvantages noted for Estrada and Estrada. Introductions to the book and to each section, plus a final selection written by two of the editors asking "What are science fiction writers trying to say to psychologists?"

Milgram, S. (ed.) (1975) *Psychology in Today's World.* Boston: Little, Brown, 387 pp. (8½ x 11 format). Seventy-seven selections from the popular press, published originally from approximately 1968 to 1974. One of the most interesting collections of this type, as might be expected from its editor, but risks giving a stamp of approval to questionable reports by reprinting such selections as one from *The Secret Life of Plants.* Although the introduction to that section ("Frontiers") does suggest that the editor is not convinced by the arguments therein, students may not notice the disclaimer. Introductions to the book and each section plus an index.

Mussen, P., Rosenzweig, M. R., and others (eds.) (1974) *Concepts in Psychology.* Lexington, Mass.: D. C. Heath, 542 pp. Thirty-seven articles from a variety of journals, each intended by the editors to represent a contemporary, significant contribution written up so as to be self-contained and not too difficult for students. These are still relatively difficult compared with some of the collections, however, being generally of the *American Scientist* level. Thus they seem useful for the editor's expressed purpose of exposing students to the functioning of modern psychological investigation and theorizing, but you should note the difference in intent and content between this and some of the other collections—for example, Milgram's or McCollom and Badore's—before choosing. Introductions to each section and to each article, original bibliographies, and an index.

Rivenbark, W. H., III, and Rosenberg, J. (eds.) (1975) *Issues in Human Behavior.* Lexington, Mass.: Xerox Individualized Publishing (XIP), 390 pp. (8½ x 11 format). Seventy-two selections from the popular press put together from XIP readers, created by individual instructors, as a "Best of XIP" reader. Introductions to the book and to each section, plus student evaluation form to provide feedback for later editions, self-review questions for each section, author and subject indexes.

Severin, F. T. (ed.) (1973) *Discovering Man in Psychology: A Humanistic Approach.* New York: McGraw-Hill, 334 pp. Somewhere between an edited reader and a text. Fifteen topics from humanistic psychology under four major categories (for example, first major category: "Underdeveloped Areas in Psychology"; first topic under it: "Love and Altruism"). Thirty-six authors, but so interspersed with editorial comment that the net result is like a text (or text outline) with extensive quotes. Suggested further readings for each topic, the original bibliographies combined into a single one, name and subject indexes.

Wertheimer, M., and Rappoport, L. (gen. eds.) (1978) *Psychology and the Problems of Today.* Glenview, Ill.: Scott, Foresman, 439 pp. Sixty-six selections from both professional and popular sources, arranged into nine "problem" sections, from "Search for Identity" to "Quality of Life," each edited by other editors. Introduction to the book by the general editors, and to each section and each selection by the section's editors, plus a single combined bibliography and an index.

Whitten, P. W. (ed.) (1977) *Being Human Today: Psychological Perspectives.* San Francisco: Canfield Press, 179 pp. (8½ x 11 format). Thirty-seven selections from the popular press. Introductions to each section.

Zimbardo, P., and Maslach, C. (eds.) (1977) *Psychology for Our Times: Readings* (2nd ed.). Glenview, Ill.: Scott, Foresman, 424 pp. (8½ x 11 format). Fifty-four selections from literary, historical, and popular sources, all bearing on aspects of psychology personally relevant to students—for example, drugs, personal identity, or sex roles. One of the most eclectic collections, with professional articles (many of them classics), excerpts from books—both professional and popular— excerpts from symposia, and so on. Introductions plus "Thought Provokers" (sets of provocative questions) for each section, plus original bibliographies.

REPRINTS

These selections from a variety of sources typically sell for substantially less than a dollar, sometimes with further discounts for quantity orders. Most require a minimum number of reprints per order, especially for purchase-order sales. For the latest arrangements contact these sources directly.

Bobbs-Merrill Reprints in Psychology. (Bobbs-Merrill Co., Inc., College Division, 4300 W. 62nd St., Indianapolis, Ind. 46206.) These include more than 750 papers in psychology reprinted from original journal articles. All are in a standard 8½ x 11 format, punched for binders. They sell direct or through bookstores and will collate and package sets of reprints at no additional charge. Individual reprints may be requested for examination, and a free instructor's copy is included, on request, for any reprint adopted in quantity. (Note that Bobbs-Merrill publishes reprints in several other relevant areas—anthropology, sociology, and so on; these are listed in separate catalogs, which are free on request to instructors.)

Psychology Today reprints. (*Psychology Today* Reprints, P.O. Box 278, Pratt Station, Brooklyn, New York 11205.) Certain of the major articles from *Psychology Today* are available. Small orders must be prepaid, including shipping and handling charges; institutional purchase orders will be accepted for large orders. They do not offer free examination copies or instructor's copies with orders. They will not collate sets of reprints, but they do offer a number of book-form reprint collections for general psychology, as well as for more specialized areas— for example, *Readings in Developmental Psychology Today.* (They also offer tape cassettes of the authors of some of these same articles discussing their subject, as is noted in Section IIC5.)

Science reprints. (American Association for the Advancement of Science, Dept. J, 1515 Massachusetts Ave., N.W., Washington, D.C. 20005.) Any article that has appeared in *Science* in the past six years can be obtained. These articles are typically too advanced for introductory courses, but this is not always true.

Scientific American reprints. (W. H. Freeman and Co., 660 Market St., San Francisco, Calif. 94104.) About 1,000 *Scientific American* articles, including several hundred specifically in psychology, are available as individual reprints and in collected form, including the one listed under "Readers" earlier and numerous specialty collections. They will collate orders of more than ten titles, if requested to do so, and will provide free examination copies on request. An indexed annotated catalog is available specifically for psychology reprints.

Warner Modular Publications. They offer selected reprints, for example, Stanley Milgram's *Human Relations* article. For other titles, write Warner Modular Publications, Inc., 11 Essex Street, Andover, Mass. 01810.

PAPERBACK MONOGRAPH SERIES

Basic Concepts in Psychology Series. (Brooks/Cole Publishing Co., 10 Davis Dr., Belmont, Calif. 94002.) These volumes were originally developed at the University of Michigan as chapters of a beginning textbook.

Abnormal Psychology, J. N. Butcher.
Animal Behavior: Theory and Research, F. J. Mortenson.
Assessment of Human Characteristics, E. L. Kelly.
Basic Statistics, W. L. Hays.
Beliefs, Attitudes, and Human Affairs, D. J. Bem.
Clinical Psychology: An Empirical Approach, E. L. Hoch.
Cognitive Processes, M. Manis.
Comparative Psychology, R. A. Maier.
Conditioning and Instrumental Learning, E. L. Walker.
Human Performance, P. M. Fitts and M. I. Posner.
Motivation: A Study of Action, D. Birch and J. Veroff.
Neuropsychology: The Study of Brain and Behavior, C. M. Butter.
Non-Freudian Personality Theories, J. Geiwitz.
Psychodynamics: The Science of Unconcious Mental Forces, G. S. Blum.
Sensory Processes, M. Alpern, M. Lawrence, and D. Wolsk.
Social Psychology: An Experimental Approach, R. B. Zajonc.
Some Thoughts About Teaching the Beginning Course in Psychology, E. L. Walker
    and W. J. McKeachie.

Foundations of Modern Psychology Series (2nd ed.). (Prentice-Hall, Inc., Englewood Cliffs, N.J. 07632.) Each volume in this series is written at the introductory level by an authority in the field.

Abnormal Psychology, S. Cashdan.
Clinical Psychology (2nd ed.), J. Rotter.
Humanistic Psychology, J. Shaffer.
Language and Thought, J. Carroll.
Learning (2nd ed.), S. Mednick.
The Nature of Physiological Inquiry, R. Hyman.
Organizational Psychology (2nd ed.), E. Schein.
Perception (2nd ed.), J. Hochberg.
Personality (2nd ed.), R. Lazarus.
Physiological Psychology: Fundamental Principles, P. Teitelbaum.
The Psychological Development of the Child (2nd ed.), P. Mussen.
School Psychology, J. Bardon and V. Bennett.
Social Psychology (2nd ed.), W. Lambert.
Tests and Measurements (2nd ed.), L. Tyler.

Insight Series. (Van Nostrand Reinhold Co., 7625 Empire Drive, Florence, Kentucky 41042.) This series consists primarily of readings and controversial papers on specific topics, but includes others.

Animal Drives, G. A. Cicala (ed.).

Anthropology: A Human Science, M. Mead.

Creativity and Conformity, C. Moustakas.

Creativity and Personal Freedom, F. Barron.

The Encapsulated Man, J. R. Royce.

The Experience of Psychotherapy: What It's Like for Client and Therapist, W. H. Fitts.

Experimental Studies of Single Cases, P. O. Davidson and C. G. Costello.

Instinct, R. C. Birney and R. C. Teevan (eds.).

Intelligence: Some Recurring Issues, L. E. Tyler.

Interpersonal Accommodation, M. Abrahamson.

Measuring Human Motivation, R. C. Birney and R. C. Teevan (eds.).

The Neurological Basis of Motivation, S. E. Glickman and P. M. Milner.

Psychological Needs and Cultural Systems, J. Aronoff.

Race, Science and Humanity, A. Montagu.

Research in Psychopathology, H. D. Quay (ed.).

Social Perception, H. Toch and H. C. Smith (eds.).

Theories of Motivation in Learning, R. C. Teevan and R. C. Birney (eds.).

Theories of Motivation in Personality and Social Psychology, R. C. Teevan and R. C. Birney (eds.).

Toward a Psychology of Being (2nd ed.), A. H. Maslow.

Perspectives in Psychology. John Wiley & Sons, 605 Third Ave., New York, N.Y. 10016.) Using a slightly different approach, these volumes combine historical selections with extensive transitional discussion by the authors.

The Child, W. Kessen (ed.).

Individual Differences, A. Anastasi (ed.).

Language and Psychology: Historical Aspects of Psycholinguistics, A. L. Blumenthal.

Visual Perception: The Nineteenth Century, W. N. Dember (ed.).

2. From the American Psychological Association (APA). (This section also is intended primarily for newcomers; those familiar with APA and its offerings may skip it.) The help that the APA can provide is of essentially two types: membership in Division Two, and several publications concerned with the teaching of psychology.

Division Two is specifically concerned with the teaching of psychology. Regardless of which other division(s) you may join based on your own area(s) of specialization, if you are teaching psychology you will probably also wish to join Division Two. They publish a journal *Teaching of Psychology*, which itself is a very useful teaching aid. This journal began with the October 1974 issue and replaces the newsletter Division Two formerly provided. An earlier issue of the newsletter, the March 1973 issue on undergraduate TAs, has already been referenced, in Section IIB9. (To join, write for information to the APA address given at the end of this section, and they will put you in touch with Division Two.)

Of the various APA publications, several are likely to be of particular use for the introductory course. One of them is the reference work familiarly known as the Red Book, formally titled *The Psychology Teacher's Resource Book: First Course* (1973). This book is currently being revised, and a new edition should be ready by 1980.

Included in the Red Book are reviews of texts, books of readings, and laboratory manuals, as well as sections on periodicals, novels, and other popular books, audio-visual materials, reference materials, equipment suppliers, addresses of national organizations concerned with psychology-related functions, and sections offering ways of increasing student involvement and of organizing instruction. The magnitude of the resources thus offered, either directly within those pages or from the listed national organizations, is enormous. You should by all means acquire a copy.

Another APA publication that you will find useful is the Gray Book, formally titled *Undergraduate Education in Psychology* (1973), a report of a three-year study of the undergraduate curriculum in psychology by the University of Michigan. Survey and field-site case-study approaches were used, to serve two goals: "to describe undergraduate education nationwide and to report on innovative approaches that may point the way to the future." Its subsections will be useful in making many of the decisions listed in Section IIB of this handbook: consideration of student and course goals, the use of laboratories, and so on. It also includes separate discussions of the problems of the introductory course at large universities, small liberal arts colleges, community colleges, and even British universities.

Other publications of interest are Johnson and Ruskin's summary of behavioral instruction, listed among the references in Section IIB10, and Maas and Kleiber's *Directory of Teaching Innovations*, noted at the end of Section I. The latter is a compilation of over 500 replies to a questionnaire on innovative programs in psychology teaching. The editors have provided extensive indexing but the programs are presented as their originators described them, complete with addresses should you wish to contact them directly.

Other APA publications that you might find useful include those produced by the APA's Journal Supplement Abstract Service (JSAS). This system is set up to publish materials included in the following categories: massive data collections, methodological techniques, educational materials, projects in progress, technical reports, fresh looks at controversial issues, demands on psychology, management of psychological resources, APA task force reports, bibliographies, information on psychology and public policy, literature reviews, well-designed studies that are "near replications," well-designed studies with negative results. Quarterly catalogs of these publications are available from the JSAS at the APA address given at the end of this section.

A publication of the JSAS that may be of interest is:

B. Singer, "A Practical Annotated Bibliography on College Teaching and the Teaching of Psychology," ms. no. 331, abstracted in the JSAS *Catalog of Selected Documents in Psychology* 3 (1973): 34. This includes references specifically oriented to problems of grading, team teaching, and so on, as well as those for college teaching and especially psychology teaching. It also includes student-oriented works, journals, and so on.

In addition, each year the December issue of *Teaching Psychology* provides an updated annotated bibliography on the teaching of psychology.

Finally, some other APA offerings may be helpful as supplements not only for your use, but for your school's counseling service or your students. They include the APA style book, the *Publication Manual*, 2nd ed., *Career Opportunities for Psychologists: Expanding and Emerging Areas*, and the pamphlets *Careers in Psychology* and *Ethical Standards of Psychologists*. All are well done and inexpensive. All these publications are available from the American Psychological Association, 1200 17th St., N.W., Washington, D.C. 20036.

3. From Other Instructors. Other instructors can be very helpful to you in a variety of ways. One way is through their published works: those included in the list at the end of Section IIC1, for example, and the APA publications noted in Section IIC2 above (especially the books listed in Singer's JSAS bibliography).

Instructors at your own school can be another valuable source of help, especially those who have taught the introductory course before. Since they are oriented to your school and its students, their tips can be especially valuable.

Access to such aid will vary by locale, however. The number of instructors in the department and the frequency and type of faculty get-togethers can influence the exchange of information, as can the particular local conventions regarding sitting in on another instructor's lectures. Unfortunately, there are often strong (although unwritten) rules against sitting in. There *are* valid reasons for this, not the least of which is the hard-to-avoid tendency for instructors to play their lectures to their visiting colleague(s) rather than to the students. But such rules do tend to close off a valuable source of information for the new instructor.

If such "observational learning" appeals to you, perhaps you could try to arrange to sit in on a particular class by agreement with the instructor. Your best bet is probably a departmental "star" performer. Such stars are not only good models but, with their reputation clearly established, are more likely to feel confident of their technique in your presence and less likely to be threatened by you.

Another way of achieving this purpose is to ask other instructors to be guest lecturers. Not only do you obtain the benefits noted in Section IIB5, but you also get to observe the guests' technique.

You should beware, however, of being unduly influenced by what other instructors in your department do. Because of the prominence of the introductory course, you will feel a pressure to meet the standards of others, either through your own wish to "measure up" or via student comments that Professor So-and-So does it this way—for example, gives exams differently, holds class differently, believes differently. While you should, of course, avoid being dogmatic, remember that it is *your* course. Diversity in the department, and especially in this course, is both inevitable and desirable.

4. From Your Students. One trend in education seems to be to provide students with more of a voice in their own education. Important information can be obtained from your students; in some cases more direct aid may also be obtained. Examples already mentioned in previous sections include the demographic characteristics of the students (obtained at the first class meeting) and the possible use of undergraduate TAs.

There are several different ways that you may obtain information from your current students within the structure of the class. They are discussed in Section V, with a focus on the evaluation of the course and the instructor, but the same procedures can be used to provide more information about students. In addition, however, you may wish to contact students *not* in your current class. A questionnaire for seniors, for example, both psychology majors and nonmajors, might bring out views of the good and bad points of the introductory course, as viewed in retrospect, which could aid your teaching of current and future versions of it.

On the other hand, a questionnaire for students in a notably popular—or unpopular—introductory course in another area might yield information valuable not only to the instructor of that course but to you. (Clearly, cooperation of the other instructor is more likely for a wildly popular course than the opposite.)

The types of assistance possible from student TAs have already been noted in Section IIB9. Students in the class can also assist with lesser support functions, however, such as passing out syllabi or other materials or helping to set up demonstrations. Such help is necessarily limited, of course; both students and your department might be expected to look askance at your using them for guest lecturers. On the other hand, don't assume that distributing passouts is all they can do. The author once allowed students in a discussion section who had studied visual perception for most of the term and had developed some good demonstrations to present them to the class as a whole; they did a pretty good job, complete with passouts. Or perhaps something developed during one term could be presented to the next term's class, at the appropriate time in the syllabus.

If properly managed, student participation in such projects can help to serve many purposes valuable for an introductory course: personal as well as academic involvement in psychology, the performing of "psychologist" behavior rather than just the observing of it, and so on. The very fact that even some students are participating in the class can be useful in motivating all students and in keeping them on your side. This can then be a valuable counter to the problem of testing, which, as noted earlier (Section IIB10), tends to turn you into "the enemy."

5. Audiovisual Aids. The use of audiovisual aids—films, slides, audiotapes, videotapes, and so on—is discussed in Section IIB6. If you choose to use any of them, there are numerous suppliers. Most such aids may be purchased or rented. Usually slides and tapes are purchased, often from major publishers. Films, however, are usually rented, most typically from the special departments set up for this purpose at major universities throughout the country. (It is desirable to have at least a limited library of films owned by the department. It may be feasible to purchase at least a few films by adjusting the budget accordingly, especially if you expect to use them regularly. Some companies recognize this and offer several-year lease-purchase agreements.) Films available at special rates from Harcourt Brace Jovanovich, Inc., are described in Section IVE and are included in the references of Section VI.

Films are available from the film departments of a number of major universities, including those listed below, as well as numerous other suppliers of different types. The best policy is probably to familiarize yourself with one or two of the university systems for general film use. As noted in the annotated list of suppliers at the end of this section, their catalogs are comprehensive and a review of any of them will familiarize you with the offerings available. For contemporary or "art" films, as opposed to those primarily designed as educational films, see the McGraw-Hill catalog. If particular films or film series with limited distribution appeal to you, you can consider the suppliers of them also.

Specific film suggestions are included in the chapter-by-chapter supplements of Section VI. But any such suggestions are necessarily a very small sample of the potentially applicable films. You may wish to obtain several of the catalogs listed below simply to note the range of materials available, even if you then select a single supplier. But keep in mind that the use of rental films involves a substantial amount of planning, ordering, and other administrative detail; dealing with more than one or two agencies can greatly increase the complexity of, and the probability of errors in, this administrative detail.

It should be recognized that these films are restricted neither to "psychology" nor to "educational" films. Available films include feature-length films (both classic and quite recent), cartoons (such as the excellent ones produced by the National Film Board of Canada and by the similar Yugoslavian group), many of the "Candid Camera" bits, film versions of famous television series, and more. Many of these are listed in the McGraw-Hill catalog. (If you can figure out how to use them, you can get a film version of the crisis-induced hallucination of Ambrose Bierce's *An Occurrence at Owl Creek Bridge*, the personality study of Mel Brooks' award-winning cartoon *The Critic*, the Academy Award-winning Yugoslavian cartoon *Ersatz*, or feature films—from Buster Keaton to *Bridge on the River Kwai*.) For ideas, you might review one instructor's use of nonpsychology films: M. Bolt, "Using Films Based on Literature in Teaching Psychology," *Teaching of Psychology* 3 (1976): 189–90. Also, although these are now becoming dated, some 200 "Candid Camera" sequences are available, for purchase only, from Du Art Film Labs. A description of the collection is presented in J. B. Maas and K. M. Toivanen, "Candid Camera and the Behavioral Sciences," *A-V Communications Review* 17 (1969): 307–14 (reprinted in *Teaching of Psychology*, 5 (1978): 226–28).

In seeking films, be sure to check the date and description carefully and, if possible, find a review in one of the references noted below. Many of the available "psychology" films with interesting sounding titles and descriptions are, in fact, abysmal films. Often they are so old as to be "camp," psychologically out of date, and in bad physical shape. Others are simply poor examples of the filmmaking art: dull, uninspired, black-and-white renditions of someone's theory, which are practically guaranteed to remove whatever interest the topic might have had for your students. (Nearly all of the films listed in Section VI are color and of 1970 or more recent vintage.)

Even if you have been careful in choosing your film, it is still wise to preview it before showing; most suppliers will arrange advance previews of films. If you cannot arrange to preview a film well in advance, to decide if you will use it in the course, at least preview it before showing it to the class. If it is *too* bad, you can lecture instead. If you do show it, a preview allows you to prepare the students to ignore some aspects, pay attention to others, consider questions not raised in the soundtrack, and so on. If these ideas only occur to you during the screening for the class, you will be less effective in trying to add them then or after the showing.

One warning is in order regarding scheduling. Popular films are often fully reserved months in advance. The ideal policy—though often hard to achieve in practice—is to place your order a term in advance. Even then you may have to accept an alternate date on some selections. If you can find a relatively local supplier, you may be able to reduce these problems to some extent. If you teach within reasonable driving distance of one of the listed suppliers, you may be able to phone them for a discussion of possible dates and in some instances may be able to rent a film on a one-day-only basis by picking it up and returning it yourself. Thus, you can sometimes get films that would not be available if they had to be mailed to you and back. Other suppliers, for example, CRM, include phone numbers of area representatives in their catalogs and can sometimes arrange last-minute showings under special circumstances.

The following list of film suppliers is not meant to be comprehensive but is intended to note the major suppliers likely to be helpful to you. For other references see the appropriate section of the APA's Red Book; it includes descriptions of notable film series, lists of films appropriate to particular topics, and so on. New films are reviewed in several publications, including *Teaching of Psychology* and *Contemporary Psychology*. Mental health films are also cataloged by NIMH (Publications and Reports Section, Office of the Directors, National Institute of Mental Health, U.S. Department of Health, Education, and Welfare, Washington, D.C. 20225). A comprehensive (and expensive) listing of audiovisuals is available in the *Index to Psychology: Multimedia* (Los Angeles, Calif.: National Information Center for Educational Media, 1972). Another comprehensive listing, giving over 700 films and 40 distributors, is *Films in the Behavioral Sciences: An Annotated Catalog* (Audio-Visual Laboratory, University of Oklahoma Medical Center, 800 N.E. 13th St., Oklahoma City, Okla. 73104). One of the most helpful and complete film guides on the market is the *Film Programmers Guide to 16 mm Rentals* (1975) by K. Weaver; it lists practically every film made by Hollywood and foreign producers. It's available from Reel Research, Box 6037, Albany, Calif. 94706. A specialized list of interest is *Films by and/or About Women* (1972), available from Women's History Research Center, Inc., 2325 Oak Street, Berkeley, Calif. 94708. A general reference of potential interest is R. H. Anderson, *Selecting and Developing Media for Instruction* (New York: Van Nostrand Reinhold, 1976).

For all of the following suppliers, film catalogs are free on request and distribution is open to all geographic areas except where noted. Most catalogs include a description of each film, including plot, time, black-and-white or color, date made, and, for some, original source (for example, full-length feature, NET-TV series). Most suppliers limit films to nonprofit educational purposes and most of them control or prohibit their use on TV systems. For those suppliers from which the author has obtained catalogs, notes are included. In several other cases, the addresses are those recommended in the APA's Red Book as major sources. (Film rental costs range from well under $10 to over $100, with most from $15 to $35. The fees tend to be proportional to length, but vary also according to supplier, original source, and so on; see the catalogs for specific prices.)

FILMS AND VIDEOTAPES

Boston University, Krasker Memorial Film Library, School of Education, 765 Commonwealth Ave., Boston, Mass. 02215.

University of California, Extension Media Center, 2223 Fulton St., Berkeley, Calif. 94720. Their frequently updated and well-organized catalog is one of the best guides to available educational films, with relatively lengthy descriptions of films. Rental distribution is limited to the United States. They also offer special newsletters on particular groups of films (for example, on the women's movement), specialized brochures (for example, ecology, drugs), and so on.

CRM/McGraw-Hill Films, 110 Fifteenth St., Del Mar, Calif. 92014. This supplier was a branch of Communications Research Machines, Inc., the publishers of *Psychology Today.* They are now affiliated with McGraw-Hill Films, and many of the CRM films are also available from McGraw-Hill, but each lists films not available from the other. (Section VI uses CRM as the primary listing, using McGraw-Hill only for those not available from CRM. See the McGraw-Hill listing below for their catalog.) Their rental charges are higher than some suppliers but the films tend to be worth it; they are all relatively new, in color, and have visual flair. Their collection includes at least 74 films. (New ones are continually being added; 19 were added in 1978 alone.) A brochure/catalog is available and brief descriptions of new films will be sent to those interested.

Du Art Film Labs, Inc., 245 W. 55th St., New York, N.Y. 10019. They are the suppliers of the "Candid Camera" films, which are for sale only.

Encyclopaedia Britannica Films, Inc., 1150 Wilmette Ave., Wilmette, Ill. 60091; 277 Pharr Road N.E., Atlanta, Ga. 30305. Their catalog lists only films produced by them, but there are 1,200 of them. They are, however, intended primarily for purchase; although they can be leased on a long-term basis, single rentals are not offered.

Harper & Row Media, 2350 Virginia Ave., Hagerstown, Md. 21740, offers a number of films of interest (see the specific listing in Section VI), including Milgram's films and others written and/or edited by a number of other well-known psychologists. Catalog also offers filmstrip and audio tapes of interviews with many of the best-known psychologists.

Harcourt Brace Jovanovich, Inc., 757 Third Ave., New York, N.Y. 10017. As described in more detail in Section IVE, they offer films specifically designed to complement *Introduction to Psychology*, 7th ed., at special rates to users of the text.

Houghton Mifflin Co., Dept. M., 110 Tremont St., Boston, Mass. 02107.

University of Illinois, Visual Aids Service, Division of University Extension, Champaign, Ill. 61822. Their catalog is enormous and is supplemented yearly and replaced every four years. A nominal charge unless you are renting films (but a free copy was, in fact, sent to the author on request). They also produce a newsletter several times a year with articles on film, reports of new films, and so on.

Indiana University, Audio-Visual Center, Division of University Extension, Bloomington, Ind. 47401. Brochure on request; charge for catalog, with latest supplement. Said by the Red Book to be an especially large collection.

University of Iowa, Audio-Visual Center, Iowa City, Iowa 52240. Another enormous catalog, published every three years, with yearly supplements. This actually represents combined services of the University of Iowa and Iowa State; details are in the catalog.

Kent State University, Audio-Visual Services, Kent, Ohio 44242. Said by the Red Book to have one of the most complete collections in the country and to offer a special issue-oriented catalog.

University of Maine, Audio-Visual Center, Orono, Me. 04473.

McGraw-Hill Films, 1221 Avenue of the Americas, New York, N.Y. 10020. As noted above, their catalog now includes many of the CRM offerings (although these are listed as CRM in Section VI), but it also offers many others, including both specifically psychology films and the others discussed in Section IiC5.

University of Michigan, Audio-Visual Education Center, 416 4th St., Ann Arbor, Mich. 48103. Another substantial catalog, again representing the combined services of two universities, the University of Michigan and Michigan State. The catalog was dated several years earlier, but came with a recent supplement.

University of Minnesota, Department of Audio-Visual Extension, General Extension Division, 2037 University Ave. S.E., Minneapolis, Minn. 55455. Another enormous university catalog. The one supplied was dated two years earlier, with no specification of how frequently it is revised; it did note that a separate publication is available containing notes on new offerings.

National Film Board of Canada, 1251 Avenue of the Americas, New York, N.Y. 10020. Many of their films are available from McGraw-Hill Films, but you may write to them directly. They have some particularly good films related to cultural differences, frequently based on Canadian Indian and French groups, as well as on emotional adjustment in general.

University of Nebraska, Great Plains National Instructional Television Library, Box 80669, Lincoln, Nebr. 68501. This catalog offers primarily videotape, in reels or video cassettes, but also includes films. Many of these video offerings are TV courses developed at other universities and available through this center. The catalog supplied was current, but the frequency of updating is not known.

New York University, Film Library, 26 Washington Pl., New York, N.Y. 10003. Said by the Red Book to have especially large and useful holdings, including a number of special series.

University of Oklahoma, Health Sciences Center, Behavioral Sciences Media Laboratory, 800 N.E. 13th St., P.O. Box 26901, Oklahoma City, Okla. 73190.

Oklahoma State University, Audiovisual Center, Stillwater, Okla. 74074. A comprehensive catalog, but very difficult to read because of very small print. The catalog supplied was intended to cover the current year and two more, with no specification of an updating system.

Pennsylvania State University, Psychological Cinema Register, Audio-Visual Aids Library, University Park, Pa. 16802. Their films are oriented only to "psychology, psychiatry, animal behavior, anthropology and related behavioral sciences." The catalog is the size of a pocketbook rather than an urban phone book, as those of Illinois and Iowa are, but this is achieved partly by very small print. The catalog supplied was dated two years earlier, but a stack of newsletters issued bi-monthly came with it for updating. This is one of the best general-purpose sources.

Prentice-Hall, Inc., Film Library, Englewood Cliffs, N.J. 07632. Prentice-Hall now offers the films formerly available from Appleton-Century-Crofts. A brochure/catalog is available.

Psychological Films, 205 West 20th Street, Santa Ana, Calif. 92706. This supplier offers a folder of descriptive sheets for its films of well-known psychologists (for example, Maslow), psychotherapists (for example, Rogers, Perls), and therapy techniques. While limited in number, some of these films are unusually interesting. (A set of three, for example, shows Rogers', Perls', and Ellis' approach to the same patient, while another set shows three approaches to group therapy.)

Research Press Films, Box 31770, Champaign, Ill. 61820. A limited number of films that are oriented specifically to the behavioral approach, including some by and/or about Albert Bandura, B. F. Skinner, and Gerald Patterson.

University of Southern California, Department of Cinema, University Park, Los Angeles, Calif. 90007. Catalog of 2,000 films (nominal charge).

University of Texas, Visual Instruction Bureau, Drawer W., University Station, Austin, Tex. 78712. Catalog (nominal charge).

University of Wisconsin, Bureau of Audio-Visual Instruction, 1312 W. Johnson St., Madison, Wis. 53715. Limited to Wisconsin and adjoining states.

AUDIOTAPES

The Red Book lists several specialty suppliers of tapes and some film suppliers also offer tapes. In addition, an increasing number of major publishers are offering tapes. Of these, one of the largest offerings is that of McGraw-Hill. Their "Sound Seminar Series" offers over 200 titles. Most of them are well-known psychologists speaking on an enormous variety of subjects, from Anna Freud's discussion of childhood aggression to Harlow's views on physiological psychology. An annotated catalog is available; write to the College Division, McGraw-Hill Book Co., 1221 Avenue of the Americas, New York, N.Y. 10020.

Jeffrey Norton is another publisher offering some interesting tapes, from E. G. Boring speaking on the "Great Man" in science (1952) to a six-hour album recorded at the two-day confrontation of Rogers and Skinner at the University of Minnesota (1962). For a catalog of over 300 cassettes, write Jeffrey Norton Publishers, Inc., Tape Department, 145 East 49th St., New York, N.Y. 10017.

Harper & Row also offers a limited number of recently recorded interviews with famous psychologists. These are included in their film catalog, available from Harper & Row Media, 2350 Virginia Ave., Hagerstown, Md. 21740.

Another source of tapes is APA. In addition to the publications noted earlier in Section IIC2, it offers "Master Lectures" in several areas of psychology, for example, physiological and developmental, taken from the special talks presented yearly at APA conventions; each is two hours long. It also offers the invited addresses from recent conventions. As with APA publications, they are available from American Psychological Association, 1200 17th Street, N.W., Washington, D.C. 20036.

Psychology Today offers tape cassettes of the authors of some recent major articles discussing their work with the *Psychology Today* editors. For a catalog, write Cassette Catalog, P.O. Box 278, Pratt Station, Brooklyn, N.Y. 11205.

Another useful tape supplier is the Pacifica Foundation. This group owns four nonprofit educational FM radio stations and has collected over 11,000 programs from their broadcasts, including lectures by famous psychologists and educators, as well as panel discussions, and so on. They can supply reels or cassettes. Write to Pacifica Tape Library, 5316 Venice Blvd., Los Angeles, Calif. 90019.

SLIDES AND TRANSPARENCIES

The most comprehensive slide sets available are those compiled by Professor James B. Maas and distributed by McGraw-Hill as "Slide Group for General Psychology (I and II)." The first set of 300 color slides (1967) offers comprehensive coverage of traditional subject areas, under ten topics: physiological basis of behavior, the senses, learning, motivation, emotion, conflict and frustration, personality, individual differences, mental illness, and social psychology. This set has already been adopted by over 1,200 colleges. The second set of 150 color slides (1974) supplements the first one, though it can be used separately. It covers six topics: psychophysiology of sleep and dreaming, instrumentation of research and demonstration of psychological phenomena, learning concepts and experimental paradigms, assessment concepts and techniques, paintings by the disturbed mind, and the emotional brain and neuropsychiatric therapies. The technical quality and the artwork are excellent and an instructor's manual accompanying each set offers clear explanatory notes for each picture. (There is also a study guide for the first set.) The sets are available from McGraw-Hill Book Co., College and University Division, 1221 Avenue of the Americas, New York, N.Y. 10020.

Another group of high-quality illustrations is provided by Henry Slucki's collection of 64 acetate transparencies: "Transparencies for General Psychology." These concentrate on four areas: physiological psychology, statistics, learning, and perception. The overlay or manipulation of interlocking sheets permits special effects of movement and measurement of such things as the extent of the Müller-Lyer illusion, variables associated with size constancy, and the nervous impulse in the afferent neuron. An instructor's manual and individual note sheets for each transparency give detailed instructions for the most effective use of the materials, as well as historical background for some topics and latest research findings for others. The full set of transparencies may be ordered from Scott, Foresman and Co., 1900 E. Lake Ave., Glenville, Ill. 60025.

A third set of general-purpose overhead transparencies for introductory psychology classes is available from Research Media, Inc. They are divided into five parts: statistics, perception, physiology, heredity, and learning; there are seven color transparencies per part. Write to Research Media, Inc., 4 Midland Ave., Hicksville, N.Y. 11801.

A variety of special-purpose slide and transparency sets are also available. (Several of the major publishers include them in their catalogs and the APA's Red Book lists some of them.) One set worth noting describes Professor Philip Zimbardo's 1971 social psychology study of a simulated prison at Stanford University. This study became nationally known, partially because of its timing—just before the Attica prison riot—and this slide set with soundtrack has been shown to public officials, prison guards, and others interested in prison reform, as well as to psychologists and students. The set of 80 slides is accompanied by a tape cassette soundtrack, which is designed for self-synchronization with the slides if the appropriate equipment is available or manual synchronization via an annotated script. The set runs 52 minutes. It is available directly from P. Zimbardo, P.O. Box 4395, Stanford, Calif. 94305.

6. Demonstration Equipment. Demonstrations and exercises that call for a minimum of equipment are suggested in the *Study Guide* accompanying the Seventh Edition. For further demonstration suggestions, see the specific ones included in the back of the APA's Red Book, or refer to one or more of the several laboratory manuals available. The Red Book also includes detailed reviews of 22 of them; the experiments included vary in complexity, subjects used, and so on, but many are adaptable for demonstration uses (especially if small sections are used). For details see the Red Book.

Equipment needed for demonstrations may be purchased as such or built up; there are numerous suppliers of both equipment and components. Again, the Red Book is a major source; it lists seven reference books for equipment building, 52 suppliers of equipment, eight references for animal care and experimentation, and 42 suppliers of animals, food, and supplies. A selected list of three publications and six major suppliers of equipment is presented below. For more details, write for catalogs; for more references, see the Red Book. (Occasional articles in *Teaching of Psychology* are also useful. See, for example, Ludy T. Benjamin, Jr., "Perceptual Demonstrations—Or What to Do with an Equipment Budget of $75" 3 (February 1976): 37–39.)

PUBLICATIONS

Guide to Scientific Instruments. (Annually, November issue) *Science.*

Instrumentation in Psychology. (1975) *American Psychologist,* Special Issue (March, 1975). New instrumentation as of 1975, including a Buyer's Guide.

National Research Council, Institute of Laboratory Animal Resources. (1972) *Guide for the Care and Use of Laboratory Animals.* (4th edition of *Guide for Laboratory Animal Facilities and Care*) Washington, D.C.: U.S. Government Printing Office.

EQUIPMENT

BRS/LVE, 5301 Holland Dr., Beltsville, Md. 20705. All forms of psychological lab apparatus, programming equipment, and so on.

Lafayette Instrument Co., P.O. Box 1279, Lafayette, Ind. 47902. Assorted behavioral, physiological, and measuring equipment, and so on.

Mogul-ED, Educational Products Div., Mogul Corp., P.O. Box 482, Oshkosh, Wis. 54901. Animals, from protozoa to mammals, and supplies, as well as models, skeletons, and so on.

Ralph Gerbrands Co., 8 Beck Rd., Arlington, Mass. 02174. Much operant research equipment, as well as polygraphs, color mixers, pursuit rotors, tachistoscopes, and so on.

Scientific Prototype Mfg. Co., 615 W. 131st St., New York, N.Y. 10027. General lab apparatus, stereotaxic equipment, video equipment, and so on.

Stoelting Co., 1350 S. Kostner, Chicago, Ill. 60623. Psychological and educational tests, finger mazes, puzzle boxes, polygraphs, plethysmographs, and so on.

III. TEACHING THE INTRODUCTORY PSYCHOLOGY COURSE

A. TIPS FOR BEGINNING INSTRUCTORS

1. Planning. One of the most strongly advised, and yet most difficult to accomplish, suggestions for teaching this course as a new instructor is to *plan*. Even with advanced planning there will be plenty of decisions and adjustments to make during the course. Without well-thought-out plans, however, you may find yourself one step ahead of chaos at all times, and may be unable to raise your sights higher than the next class meeting for the entire term. Section II of this handbook is the most specifically oriented to planning, but Sections III, IV, and VI are also likely to be helpful to you.

Section II goes into detail on the problems, decisions, and resources involved in planning your course. Section IIA alerts you to aspects of the typical introductory psychology course and its students that you will want to take into account in your planning. Section IIB notes various decisions to be made—many of them before the course begins—and others for which prior planning is helpful, although perhaps not necessary. Section IIC lists some of the major resources available to you to aid in planning and teaching the course.

Section III offers suggestions primarily oriented to teaching the introductory course. These sections may be helpful in planning but are also intended to be reference sections to which you can return as the course is progressing. This section (that is, IIIA) is intended to offer overall suggestions to the new instructor, whereas Section IIIB offers some tips to the experienced instructor new to introductory psychology. Section IIIC offers miscellaneous and rather more detailed suggestions specifically concerned with discussion sections.

Section IV describes *Introduction to Psychology*, Seventh Edition, and its associated *Study Guide, Mastery Study Guide,* and *Test Item File* in some detail. If you are not already familiar with the previous edition of *Introduction to Psychology*, you may not be interested in how the Seventh Edition differs from the Sixth Edition, but you should be even more concerned than the instructor experienced in using the book with noting the intended goals and structure of these supplements and with the suggestions for using them.

Section VI offers chapter-by-chapter teaching supplements, which are likely to be of most help in planning particular class meetings rather than the overall course.

As suggested above, planning does not stop with the beginning of the course. Plan each day and each week, insofar as you can. If you are going to use passouts, for example, plan to write them in time to be typed and reproduced. The same, of course, applies to exams. If you use films, plan not only when you will show them, but how; arrange for projectors, screens, and assistance if necessary.

One aspect of your planning, not noted before, should be considered. Students often take introductory psychology in hopes of better understanding themselves. This is fine; however, some students will be taking the course not out of general interest but because of severe psychological problems. In offering to talk to students during office hours and in lecturing on abnormal psychology, you should plan what to do if students come to you with psychiatric problems. You will probably want to check into your school's counseling system and obtain a reference to an outside therapist if you feel that the counseling resources might not be adequate. When discussing abnormal psychology, you will also probably want to warn against the "medical student's syndrome"—the tendency of students to see in themselves the problems they read about—to avoid having to deal with students who, in fact, do not have real problems. It is also a good idea to make your own specialty known to students, perhaps as a part of a general discussion of areas of psychology; when you get to abnormal psychology there will be less chance of their turning to you for "therapy." (If you *are* a clinician, you're on your own.)

One way of organizing your plans is to develop a comprehensive syllabus for distribution to students at the beginning of the course. Include notes on virtually all the decisions you have made (for example, those listed in Section IIB) and a complete schedule of class meetings, with topics, readings, exams, and so on. Developing the syllabus forces you to put everything together in a single readable package. Doing so helps you to structure the course and the end product saves you and your students time and misunderstandings once the course begins. (Students have been known to list such a syllabus as one of the things they especially liked about a course.)

In preparing the syllabus and the planning behind it, you should consider your position concerning attendance at your lectures. While some students will attend unless you drive them away and others will not unless forced to, many of those in the middle will attend more or less, as you make it more or less important and/or interesting to do so. You will have to decide how much to force attendance, via exam questions from lectures, and so on. The days before and after holiday weekends are particularly difficult. If you are trying to require attendance, you may wish to schedule important events then—for example, exams; if not, that is obviously the worst time to schedule such events. The students at your school may prefer exams before breaks, so as to be able to relax, or after breaks, so as to be able to study for them—or, more likely, some will prefer one and some the other. These preferences, if any, will simply be among the factors entering into your scheduling of exams.

You will probably also want to consider the student view in other aspects of your planning and course administration, whether out of a genuine concern for them or only a more selfish concern about the problems that dissatisfied students can cause you. (Section IIB11 discusses decisions regarding these issues; Section V considers in detail the purposes and systems for student evaluation.) One general suggestion for obtaining and keeping student good will is to be explicit and follow through. Plan not only what you will do, but how the students are to know what is expected of them. The comprehensive syllabus suggested above is one way of doing this, as is the use of a sample exam (as suggested in Section IIB10).

When you have taught the course a few times, you will be much more in control. But especially this first time, try to organize and plan as much as possible as early as possible. Your plans will still never be perfect; however much you plan, there will probably be a few things to deal with as you go along. But if you don't plan, each day will be filled with such things.

2. Getting Help. The introductory psychology course, as described in Section IIA, is typically large, multipurposed, and may contain features not found in other psychology courses, such as responsibility for the experimental-subject pool. Consequently you will need all the help that you can get.

Many people can help. Try to make friends—and stay friends—with secretaries, duplication equipment operators, and any other support personnel; you will need their help. Call on other faculty members for their help when you can: as guest lecturers, for suggestions about particular course elements, as assessors of your lecturing, and so on. (Sections IIB5, IIC1, and IIC3 include discussion of the help other instructors can offer. Note also the books listed at the end of Section I for general reference.)

If you can enlist the aid of TAs, do so. They can help you not only in exam scoring, for example, but in exam creation (although they sometimes have a tendency to create difficult, esoteric, or jargonistic items that must be counteracted with a certain amount of tact). They may even be able to set up demonstrations for you, or aid in other meaningful ways. (See Sections IIB9 and IIIC.) Your introductory psychology students can also help by providing feedback, in addition to performing more prosaic duties such as distributing your passouts. (See Sections IIC4 and VB1.)

Inanimate equipment can also help. Films, slides, audiotapes, videotapes, and demonstration equipment can help you present points, save your voice, fill in where your own knowledge is weak, and stimulate and motivate students (Sections IIB6, IIC5, IIC6, and IVE); videotape equipment can help you and your TAs evaluate your own teaching (Section VB1).

3. Lecturing. One specific area in which planning will pay off is in lectures. As noted in Section IIB5, you will want to decide what your lectures are to do, in terms of course goals, how close to the text they will be, whether passouts will be used, and so on. As also noted, you will want to blend them with films, guest lecturers, and demonstrations. Assuming that you have done that, then how do you go about the lecturing process?

The first thing to do is to organize what you want to do in each lecture. Creating your syllabus helps you to pick the topic for each lecture, but then you need to plan exactly what will be done. One way of preparing is to set up a file drawer for the course, with separate folders for each day or each concept area. Then you can insert notes, passouts, film ideas, and so on, as you think of them and compile and structure each when you can.

In doing this detailed planning, as has been noted elsewhere in this handbook, remember that your interest and enthusiasm—or lack of it—are well conveyed to students as something almost independent of the specific content of the lecture. Ideally, you have avoided the worst problems by covering the areas you are least interested in via guests or movies. But of necessity you will still be lecturing on areas outside your own specialty, some of which may not be very interesting to you. Perhaps you can find the interesting material in those areas or add something you are interested in that is appropriate. After all, if you can't find anything interesting in the material, how can you expect students to?

One way of maintaining student interest is to maintain the "relevance" level of your lectures. This is a rather overused term currently, but in this case it is expressive. Remember, your students have *no* previous psychology (presumably, since this is the introductory course). If you go immediately into the scientific method itself, you are throwing away a valuable asset: the personal relevance. Instead, try to show them how the search for valid information about behavior—for example, why their roommate behaves in some particularly bizarre way—necessarily requires controlled observation, hypotheses, and so on. They are naive about formal psychology but like all of us have a strong interest in its subject matter. If you can relate the two, you have a powerful motivation on your side.

A way of doing this, which students usually find very appealing, is to use aspects of your own life to demonstrate relevance. (This assumes that you are comfortable in doing so. It is suggested below that you should develop your own "style," and how much of yourself you wish to "expose" in this way is likely to be one variable aspect of personal style.)

Other ways of developing relevance include the use of newspaper clippings where appropriate, reference to related TV shows, the discussion of psychological aspects of campus or national controversies, and so on. A good way of involving students is to pose provocative questions, either in a batch at the first of the term for consideration later, or individually at the beginning of a lecture (or both). (See the suggestions included in Section VI. For other ideas, see the references at the end of Section I and the teaching books included in Singer's JSAS bibliography listed in Section IIC2.)

Another aspect of lecture planning, which is different from planning written materials, concerns the desired redundancy in presenting material via lectures. Just how much redundancy is desirable for your particular combination of topics and students is something that you will develop with practice. In the meantime, remember the old saw: "Tell them what you're going to tell them, tell them, then tell them what you've told them." The redundancy implied is really necessary. Unlike the printed page, lectures cannot be rescanned; it's up to you to run the important points past them again—and again, if necessary. You can do this by rephrasing, by summarizing, or by involving students in question and answer sessions.

Yet another aspect of lecture planning for the introductory course concerns the change in level of sophistication of the students as the term progresses. While this one course obviously does not make them psychologists, it can increase their knowledge dramatically. Don't be so impressed by the comments made at various places in this handbook (for example, Section IIA1) as to how naive your students will be that you treat them the same way throughout the term. If your course is at all successful, it will be not only possible but desirable to increase the level of sophistication of your lectures as you go along, building on earlier material in your coverage of the later topics.

Enough of lecture planning. What of lecturing itself, the delivery of what you have planned? First of all, it is probable that the major problem in lecturing for the beginning instructor will be speaking at all under the circumstances. The magnitude of "stage fright" anxiety effects may not be recognized by the inexperienced. If you have lectured, you almost certainly are aware of this already. While some people may be able to manage without difficulty, they are rare. For most, lecturing to a large class is rather like parachuting: The first trick is just to be able to do it—the finesse comes later. Planning helps but will not eliminate this effect. Mercifully, practice does seem to eliminate it, though faint residuals may appear as much as several terms or even years later. It would probably also help to have an over-learned lecture to present, but it is unlikely that a new instructor will have any such lecture, much less enough of them for the entire course.

Probably the best procedure is to know your lecture plan reasonably well and then to prepare simple outline-form notes. These can not only act as cues but also, by noting particular terms, dates, and diagrams crucial to the presentation, can help avoid those awful periods of blankness that can strike under the pressure of the situation, leaving you unable to remember the term that you have just assured the class is crucial to an understanding of the topic. You may wish to put some of this detail on the board, either before you begin the class or as you go along. It helps students get the correct spelling and, if any outline is included, helps them structure their notes in the way you find appropriate. You do run some risk, however, if extensive notes are put up before the lecture. Students will work at copying them and can easily miss your introductory remarks completely. (It would be easier for both you and them to put extensive notes into a passout.)

Eye contact is a nonacademic element of lecturing that often causes problems for new instructors. Probably the best bet is to move your eyes at reasonably frequent—but not frantic—intervals, stopping to make firm eye contact with students and covering the entire lecture hall (assuming that you can see that far). This lets the students see you as a person, helps keep them awake and at least seeming to pay attention, and provides you with valuable feedback about how you are coming across. Some instructors like to pick out a few students, as the term progresses, to act as representatives: "If *he* seems to understand it, everybody does," or "If *she* looks perplexed, the rest of the class is absolutely baffled." The author's preference is to "keep moving," trying to integrate all the available expressions into some sort of Gestalt.

Handling in-class questions can be another tricky problem. You will probably want to encourage active curiosity, but not to waste time or bore the class; striking a balance is up to you. Your policy on questions should be made explicit, assuming that you have one, and there are several specific caveats you should be aware of. It is important to realize, for one, how easily you may "punish" questioners if you miss the question, gloss over it, or even criticize them for asking it; unless you are careful, what you intend as a gentle return to the central issue may come out as a sharp put-down. If you are going to be willing to answer questions at all, then spend the energy and time to be sure that you have the question right and to give it a fair answer.

Starting and stopping lectures and changing topics can also be a problem until you learn how to do it. The trick here is to plan definite cues and use them explicitly and reliably. Set up one or more standard cues for starting and stopping your lecture and don't give them unless you mean it. For starting the lecture, for example, you might step up to the podium and clear your throat (or shout, depending on the size and activity level of your group), whereas for stopping you might say something specific or close your notes and step away. What you want to especially avoid is giving out ending cues early. If you say something about "Next time we will . . . ," and so on, any time in the latter half of the class, you are likely to find students closing their books and putting on their coats before you can finish the sentence. Changing topics need not be so stereotyped, but it will help your students if you make such shifts very explicit. If you shift gears without being definite about it, you can easily confuse a substantial portion of the class.

As soon as you feel ambitious enough to attempt it, however, you will want to move on from these basics and develop your own "style" in lecturing—where style implies both "mode" and "class." This may be as early as your first teaching term or only after you have successfully taught a few times, but it should come, if you intend to be professional in teaching.

As a part of developing your own style (though only a part), you should consider the use of humor. Its value as a student involver is unquestioned, but it needs to be in a form that is yours to be really effective. The University of Southern California has experimented with ways of helping its teachers be more interesting lecturers, including the use of professional gag writers. One professor, whose typical student evaluations were very low, was applauded at the end of a lecture that included professionally written "gags." USC has sought extensive foundation grants for this project, but there's no reason why you can't work on your own delivery. (This project has been widely noted. See, for example, H. Lancaster, "Ever Hear the One About the Professor and the Gag Writer?" *Wall Street Journal*, 17 April 1974, and "Cues for Tired Teaching," *Psychology Today*, July 1974, p. 25.)

An involver of even more possible value, but with more pitfalls as well, is sex. If your school, your class, and you are all comfortable with it, by all means use sexual references where appropriate. You will want to be careful of offending students (or faculty/administration), either with the sex itself or by being too sex*ist* in your remarks. A little can go a long way here, both for you and against you. Used carelessly, it can get you into trouble. But handled with discretion, this topic of perennial interest to all of us can be very useful to you and helpful to your students, by maintaining their interest and attention.

Another way of maintaining student interest is to actively involve them in the lecture. Interspersed brief demonstrations with student subjects can do this, as can questions posed to the students, with their answers noted for comparison with the real data (for example, Stanley Milgram's obedience data). Developing a set of such techniques and blending them with the other suggestions given—eye contact, questions, humor, and so on—will provide you with your own style.

Such a style can be used to effectively put across any particular content. While it has been fashionable at times to knock such deliberate development of style as phony and nonacademic, such criticism seems worse than useless, in that it inhibits active seeking of effective presentation techniques. Style without content may, in fact, be very convincing, and there is no doubt that such a procedure is dishonest. But content without style may not be very convincing at all, and content not transmitted is content wasted. (For an example of style without content, see the *Wall Street Journal* article noted above. As a separate study at USC, a professional actor used a number of style gambits to cloak nonsense content, yet greatly impressed an audience of mental health professionals. Just think of what he could have done with real content.)

One final general warning regarding lecturing. As has been noted before, your own interest or lack of interest in a subject comes through clearly to students. So try not to let fatigue, preoccupation with your own problems, or other noncurricular aspects influence your presentation. It doesn't matter whether you are really interested if the message conveyed is one of indifference or antipathy.

Overall, remember that in practical terms it is impossible to overprepare for lecturing. Professor E. L. Walker states this very well in what he terms the first law of the lecture, or Walker's Law: "No matter how hard you try, some lectures will stink. If you do not try very hard, they will all stink." (Walker and McKeachie, as listed at the end of Section I).

4. Exams and Grading. As a new instructor, you should recognize from the outset that the effects of testing and grading are deeply woven into the fabric of your course almost regardless of your particular decisions about them. From your point of view the exams should be reliable and valid measurements of student achievement, suitable for the basis of your grade reports to your school. Some of your effort will thus be spent in achieving these ends. On the other hand, from the students' point of view the exams are likely to be traumatic obstacles, to be feared and hated. As the perpetrator, you risk being tarred with the same brush. Overstated? Yes, a bit, but worth considering.

Overall, you will want to make the exams you use serve your testing purposes, but without alienating students. Section IIB10 discusses some of the possible complications in doing so. That material need not be repeated here; as part of this discussion you should read that section. Other suggestions for achieving these ends —testing while retaining student involvement and good will—include use of student feedback (see Section IIIA5), attempting to be fair in your testing and grading practices (and letting students know you are), and so on.

Some specific testing suggestions include providing a sample exam or using numerous shorter exams, as discussed in Section IIB10. You can use the *Study Guide*, the *Mastery Study Guide* or some other system to prepare the students for the exams. You can also, perhaps as part of a pre-exam review session, provide them with some tips for taking such exams—possibly even giving them duplicated review sheets specifically geared to that exam. If you feel up to it you can even attempt to explain why exams may not test on the most central facts (that is, everyone should know them and little "information" is provided to you) or why a relatively large number of questions is desirable. (Would they want to be graded on three questions, with three correct being A, two being B, and so on?)

For further general aid in exams and grading, note the McKeachie and Walker and McKeachie references at the end of Section I and the several references at the end of Section IIB10, as well as the specific suggestions in Section IVD.

5. Using Feedback. One final thought: A well-tested psychological finding indicates that improvement in performance depends critically on feedback. This process is as important for the instructor as it is for the student, and there are several different ways of getting feedback on your progress in teaching the course. As noted in Section IIIA3, you can get valuable feedback from students during the actual process of lecturing. For more quantitative or longer-term feedback from students you can use evaluation systems of a variety of sorts, as noted in Section IIB11 and in detail in Section VB. If you use them, TAs can be a valuable source of feedback (Sections IIB9 and VB), as can other instructors (Sections IIB5 and IIC3).

What matters is that you seek feedback and are responsive to it. The fact that most of this feedback is evaluative is its strength; you need to know how you are doing. But it can also be a problem; new instructors in particular typically are hesitant about being evaluated on their performance and even the simplest rating form is likely to seem threatening. It is important to remember, however, that the only reason for soliciting student response is to improve teaching. No one is a "born teacher," and many instructors have had virtually no experience before facing their first class. A wide variety of teaching styles, techniques, and materials are open to the instructor; to choose realistically among them and to capitalize on one's particular strengths or talents, frequent feedback from peers and students is essential. Remember, however, that you cannot expect to be all things to all students. Seek inputs but don't be overly concerned with trying to follow all of them at once.

B. TIPS FOR EXPERIENCED INSTRUCTORS NEW TO INTRODUCTORY PSYCHOLOGY

1. New Problems. However much experience you may have had with other more specialized courses, you will find new problems with the introductory course. In some ways your greater experience itself may *cause* problems—that is, if you attempt to treat the students and the course in the same way you do more advanced ones.

The sources of most of these problems are noted in Sections IIA1 and IIA2: the heterogeneity of the students and the multiplicity of the purposes to be served. Section IIA3 notes specific differences from more advanced courses, not only those arising from the heterogeneity of students and multiplicity of purposes, but others indigenous to the course, such as the large number of students, the use of discussion sections, and the likely inclusion of the experimental-subject pool. Much of Section IIA3, in fact, discusses the problems you will face as an experienced instructor teaching the introductory course for the first time. The material will not be duplicated here; you are urged to read that section.

2. Finding the Solutions. Once you understand where you are likely to face problems, you may use the resources in this handbook and the other works listed here for help, on a selective basis. You are not likely to have problems just giving a lecture, for example, as the new instructor may. But having realized that the lectures for this course ideally should be broader, shallower, and perhaps more "pop" than those you are used to giving, you may wish to note some of the suggestions given in Section VI for each chapter. For elements of the course that are completely unfamiliar, as discussion sections may be, for example, read the appropriate "decision" portion of Section IIB for the decisions involved (for example, IIB9 for sections). Then check Section IIC for any additional resources that may be useful. Although fully familiar with the APA, for example, you may never have paid much attention to the Red Book or the Gray Book as highly valuable references for the introductory course. (For the specific issue of discussion sections, note also the detailed consideration in Section IIIC.)

For further information and other course management suggestions, note the books listed at the end of Section I.

64

C. TIPS FOR DISCUSSION SECTIONS

1. Discussion Versus Other Sections. There are essentially four types of sections that may be used in introductory psychology: general support (that is, review of lecture and text material), special support (for example, Keller-plan testing), laboratory, and discussion. The first has some merit but probably not enough to allow it to preclude the others. The second is a specialized system. The general outlines of the plan are presented in Sections IIB10 and IVC of this handbook; details can be found in the references included there. For the third, you are advised to seek out the references given in Sections IIB9 and IIC6.

On the subject of discussion sections, however, some tips may be offered. These are by no means all-inclusive and may not be perfectly appropriate to conditions at your particular school. But you may find them both a useful introduction to the questions and helpful in seeking your own answers. Note that some of the following may be applicable to other types of sections—for example, laboratories—but that it is up to you to seek out the relevant passages.

2. Purposes Served by Discussion Sections. One of the first choices you must make is to define the purposes you wish your discussion sections to serve. The following categories might be considered. Obviously they are not mutually exclusive; on the contrary, your problem will be how to combine as many as possible.

    a. Choice
        (1) Element of choice itself
        (2) Reading about some specialized area of psychology of one's own choosing
    b. Interaction
        (1) Personal contact itself (with TA and other students)
        (2) Personalized learning from a TA (including immediate feedback on questions, modeling, and so on)
        (3) Learning from other students (for example, in discussions or class presentations)
    c. Information
        (1) Content of topic—for example, "problems in computer-assisted learning" (from reading, TA, and other students, probably in that order of importance)
        (2) Content of advanced psychology courses (to the extent the topic covers one—for example, social psychology)

(3) Learning about learning (from doing papers, class presentations, discussions, and so on—essentially a feedback process)

(4) Philosophy of psychology, experimental design and ethics, and so on (from TA, both as a data source and as a model)

(5) Back-up for the main course, both in content (questions, review before exams, and so on) and in administrative matters

Many problems in section design and administration revolve around the difficulties of satisfying combined purposes. For example, the most "content" is learned by extensive reading and the TA lecturing, with several structured papers. But this becomes a "mini-course" within the main course—presumably the function of advanced courses or directed reading—while diminishing the personal and interactive elements of a discussion section. (Note that many students *want* the mini-course and find it more difficult and frustrating to participate in discussion sections; yet at least some of these students enjoy and appreciate the latter if they are successfully brought off.)

3. Organizing the Sections. The administrative problems in handling the breakdown into sections seem to occupy much time and effort however it is done. A workable system of generating uniform sections of manageable size, with both students and TAs getting their own choice of topic to some extent, is a difficult but necessary part of any section system; the system must be carefully planned for efficiency and strongly adhered to.

Numbers are the first problem. If TAs are plentiful, you may be able to choose an ideal section size—perhaps in the range of 6 to 12 students—and obtain the help of enough TAs to do the required number of sections. More likely, the TAs will have to do more than one section and the size will still be larger than you or they would wish. (Using undergraduate TAs may be one possible way of overcoming this problem; see Section IIB9.)

Maximizing choices is the second problem. When choice of topic is an integral part of a discussion section scheme, as it often is, you cannot simply assign students to sections. Most probably you will create some scheme for choosing section topics and allowing volunteers to sign up for the sections. There are at least two basic options in setting topics and sorting students:

a. Student choice, TAs forced to fit (students choose from a list of possible topics and the resulting sections are taken by TAs on a quasi-volunteer basis);

b. TA choice, students forced to fit (TAs choose own research area or another of interest, from a list or completely arbitrarily, and the students' choice is limited to the resulting sections).

The problem is that with the first option, TAs are forced to take sections in which they are not properly prepared and/or interested; with the second, TAs may choose topics too advanced or esoteric for introductory psychology students unless they are restrained in some way.

Of these two options, it is most important that TAs have some choice. Knowledgeable and enthusiastic TAs may be able to interest reluctant students, whereas lackadaisical or disgruntled TAs are probably worse than none at all, capable of eliminating what interest students may have had in the topic.

You may best implement such a system by making up a list of acceptable section topics and readings as a guide and then letting your TAs choose on this basis, though not necessarily directly from the list. (Feedback of good and bad experiences over several quarters would probably help establish the topics or kinds of topics that are successful; see Section VB for evaluative systems, including feedback systems.) To minimize TA workloads, TAs should not be asked to prepare in areas unfamiliar to them and preferably not to prepare two different topic areas. In choosing or approving TA choices of readings, remember that arousing interest in beginning students is a common goal of sections and required reading should involve and stimulate students, even if it is not suitable as advanced reading. This is not suggesting that students be encouraged to read trash—only books that might seem too "glib," "simple," or "pop" for formal academics, the kinds of books McCollom calls "thrillers" (see reference in Section IIB7). Depending on the choice of readings, the amount of credit and time allowed for the sections, and so on, it may be possible to upgrade the reading within a single term. Sections could begin with a single "pop" paperback, for example, and progress to a more difficult work such as a second book or selections from professional journals.

4. Number and Length of Section Meetings. Sections should probably run the entire length of the course, meeting at least once a week for at least an hour. (Surprising as it may seem to some, students who do become involved often express a desire for more and longer meetings.) If it didn't raise excessive scheduling problems, the best system for section time might be to schedule rooms for two hours and let the termination of each meeting be handled by the individual sections, with time after the basic hour optional and flexible. Many students have been very disappointed when a section discussion did "come alive" only to be "killed by the bell," as it were, and some meetings will always run overtime if other classes are not scheduled in the same rooms immediately afterward.

5. Papers, Optional Work, and Supplements. The most common form of work output in sections is likely to be papers, but there are other possibilities. If you require papers, several brief ones are probably best; they help the students and the TAs learn more about each other and provide for improvement over time. In addition, a greater number of topics can be covered. TAs should be encouraged to write comments on papers, both for feedback to the students and for TA experience, even if the section is graded pass/fail.

Other forms of optional work suggested by students and TAs in the author's experience have included cooperative projects, class presentations, and dream diaries (for a Jung section). Such efforts can be valuable, but only if the TAs and the students are interested. They could be allowed at TA discretion, but all students should probably not be required to do such optional work, especially when it is personally intrusive—as dream diaries might be, for example. (Even those who do not actively participate, however, are likely to be interested and involved spectators.)

Several forms of section "supplements" have also been tried, often with positive response. Any demonstrations, films, visits to laboratories, and so on, that can tie the academic experience to "reality" are desirable. Surprisingly, many students have even listed required experimental participation as valuable, usually labeling it in some way compatible with the "reality-contact" noted above. (For experiments to be an adequate learning experience, of course, it is necessary to include an adequate debriefing, including not only removal of any deception and a statement of what was intended, but also a few comments about experimental design and problems, if appropriate.)

6. Teaching Your TAs. A problem in graduate education in psychology is that students are often taught to *be* psychologists of a particular variety, but are less likely to be taught to *teach* psychology, even though many of them will. (See J. E. Williams and C. L. Richman, "The Graduate Preparation of the College Professor: A Survey," *American Psychologist* 26 (November 1971): 1000–09.) You may even be experiencing the consequences of that situation yourself, if you are a new instructor beginning your teaching career with introductory psychology. (This handbook is, to a large extent, structured to aid in this problem.)

You can now, however, help to break that cycle if you have TAs, by helping them do as good a job as possible. It is obvious that only in this way can the TA process best serve the education of both the introductory students and the TAs, yet it is often ignored. All concerned—students, TAs, and you—will probably benefit if you expend the extra energy to help. Hold one or more TA meetings, for example, far enough in advance for TAs to choose their topics, for book ordering to be done, if necessary, and for you and TAs to discuss potential problems and your plans for them. At future meetings you can discuss the problems actually encountered and steps taken, successfully or unsuccessfully. (After the first few weeks, you may not need to hold many TA meetings, but the early ones are crucial.)

You may offer specific suggestions to your TAs in these early meetings, or you may make this handbook available to them. The following suggestions are addressed directly to TAs. A list similar to this one, with your own additions or modifications to suit your course, would probably be a valuable passout for them.

a. In choosing topic and readings, title your section to be exactly what you intend. (Some general topics can go in several directions depending on readings and TA; when sections include students expecting different directions, it is hard to compromise.)

b. Prepare in advance of each meeting a loose structure of topics desirable to cover, possible questions for use when discussion lags, and so on. Avoid the extremes of no plan or a rigid one.

c. Plan to use supplements, as noted in Section IIIC5, whenever possible.

d. Decide on a plan of lecture versus discussion. The best position is a compromise, but some topics and TA preferences will imply more of one or the other. (It may be easier to have more "lecture" earlier in the quarter, with more discussion as students acquire more information.)

e. At the first meeting, try to set the tone for later ones. Use specific "ice-breaking" techniques, note to what extent you intend to lecture and/or play the expert, note the relatively high "opinion" content in psychology as a science, and in other ways try to relieve students' anxiety about speaking out in discussion. (Fear of being "wrong" or of their opinions being of no value, especially if coupled with grading of performance, seem to be the major inhibitors of discussion.)

f. As sections progress, they will go off in their own directions. Be flexible, both within meetings and from one to the next, retaining some direction but also letting them shift. This flexibility—but with guidance—is an important part of a good discussion section.

g. In preparing questions for discussion and for paper topics, be sure they are relevant to any readings you have assigned. (If nothing in class seems very related to the readings, few are motivated to read and those few are then disappointed in the discussion.)

h. Note and keep track of aspects of the sections that you feel could be informative to the instructor or later TAs; provide them for the instructor via your local feedback system (see Section VB).

(TAs can probably also benefit from other portions of this handbook and the references included in it—especially McKeachie and Walker and McKeachie—listed at the end of Section I.)

7. Grading of Sections. The problems of grading in the sections are fairly complex. Not only must the grading serve an evaluative or feedback function for the students and for you, it must be done by TAs who are themselves students; some of them find the task even more disturbing and troublesome than you do, and others take little responsibility. Specific problems that arise are whether the sections are letter graded or only pass/fail, and why, as well as what criteria are to be used in grading. One decision that must also be made, of course, is how much of the course grade the section grade is to count.

Grading sections on a letter grade basis allows students to be graded in another way than through objective tests and provides grading experience for TAs. However, the problems of consistency of curves used by TAs, as well as definition and communication of grading standards, and so on, put a substantial burden on TAs and may work out to be unfair to many students, nonetheless. The problem with setting a firm curve and enforcing its use is that voluntary choice of sections and the small size of each section makes them very unlikely to be, in fact, equal distributions of A and B students; the strict enforcement of such a curve is thus not justified. (If letter grades are used, however, some guidelines for TAs are better than none.)

One way out is to use pass/fail grading. For this grading to have any meaning, of course, the possibility of failing should remain real.

Whether TAs give letter grades or pass/fail grades, definite standards for grading should be set by the TAs, either as a group or individually. A major decision to be made is whether or not "participation" will be graded. On the one hand, grading has an inhibiting effect on the quality of discussion; on the other hand, specific elimination of such grading removes a major input to reasonable section grading. When sections are required, this latter choice has the further effect of allowing some students not interested in discussion to make little attempt to participate.

This problem leads to the "philosophy of education" quandary of whether or not you coerce students to do something that at least some of them (who would not have volunteered) will appreciate later. If you do, some will be forced to do onerous work to no benefit of theirs and to the detriment of others through their negative effect on class discussion. If you do not, you fail to even try to reach those who might respond favorably if given some help. The percentage of the course grade allotted to the section becomes important here. Even if you encourage TAs to force attendance, it will be ineffective for some students unless the section counts for a substantial fraction of their grade. For this purpose—forcing attendance—letter grades may be more useful than pass/fail, because of the greater range of possible grades.

The author's experimentation with self-grading as one element in section letter grades, intended to provide some opportunity for student self-evaluation, seemed to be of little value. While students may be the best judge of what *they* have done, they know grades are competitive and don't know what others have done. They varied in their response to self-evaluation, sometimes giving themselves "A for effort," often refusing the option of self-grading, sometimes even giving themselves worse grades than the TA would have given them. While some students did specifically express their appreciation for the opportunity to evaluate their own work, more seemed reluctant or unconvinced. (Of course, if pass/fail grading is used, the question is academic.)

IV. USING INTRODUCTION TO PSYCHOLOGY
AND ITS SUPPLEMENTS

A. THE SEVENTH EDITION OF
INTRODUCTION TO PSYCHOLOGY

1. Goals. *Introduction to Psychology* is intended to be comprehensive, that is, to cover the entire field of psychology without undue emphasis on specialized topics. Since such a text cannot, of course, cover *all* possible topics within a single book of manageable size, it must necessarily represent some selection on the part of the authors. They have sought, however, to provide an up-to-date and balanced coverage of the major issues in psychology, giving consideration to both established areas and new developments. Topics that are especially troublesome and controversial are highlighted as such and the opposing views specifically given, but the intent has been to give a similarly balanced, though less detailed, presentation of all issues.

Introduction to Psychology is not intended to be "encyclopedic" in the sense of discrete groupings of facts, however. The arrangement of chapters as well as their content is intended to integrate knowledge of psychology rather than to fragment it. The result is a text that is deliberately comprehensive and eclectic, yet integrated—with due consideration for differing contemporary viewpoints and for theory as well as fact.

2. Structure and Features. *Introduction to Psychology* is structured around eight major sections, of one to four chapters each, for a total of 18 chapters. Statistical issues are elaborated in the single appendix. An extensive glossary, a combined list of references and index to authors cited, and a conventional index are included. Each chapter begins with a list of contents and ends with a summary of the major points included and an annotated list of suggested further readings.

The chapters as arranged are intended to provide a complete coverage of the topics typically considered in a broad and general introductory course. They are written so as to be relatively independent, however, and can be used selectively. For the same reason, they can also be used out of sequence if desired, though retaining the sequence is preferable.

Continued in the Seventh Edition of *Introduction to Psychology* is the presentation of psychological issues from five perspectives. These five approaches— *neurobiological, behavioral, cognitive, psychoanalytic,* and *phenomenological* or *humanistic*—are introduced in the first chapter and used where appropriate throughout the text. These five approaches provide the instructor with structured ways of pointing out the relationships among the various topics, as well as some of the bases for controversies that arise when investigators approach the same topic differently. Thus, they provide a means of unifying an otherwise loose federation of topics, particularly when chapters are assigned in an order other than that in which they appear in the text.

Certain unresolved and controversial issues in psychology have been treated in special Critical Discussions, separated from the body of the text. By so treating the controversial topics, these Critical Discussions prevent the book from appearing dogmatic on issues about which there is disagreement and allow the authors to present in the text what they judge to be the most plausible position without the need for qualification at every point. They believe that a textbook should have a consistent viewpoint, but it should not try to present psychology as a finished science nor defend a particular viewpoint as though it were the last word.

3. Differences from the Sixth Edition. If you are already familiar with the Sixth Edition of *Introduction to Psychology*, you will find that several aspects of the Seventh Edition are new. The major changes are noted below.

One chapter (Chapter 9 of the Sixth Edition) has been dropped, with some of the contents being distributed to other chapters. Four chapters (Chapters 8, 10, 18, and 19 of the Sixth Edition) have been completely rewritten, so that most of the content is new, and a number of other chapters have been extensively rewritten. One chapter (Chapter 14 of the Sixth Edition) has been moved earlier in the sequence.

Notable changes are presented below, by chapter. For all chapters numbered 9 and above, the equivalent Sixth Edition chapter number is included in parentheses.

Chapter 1: In this introductory chapter, the humanistic approach is now called "phenomenological or humanistic" (and phenomenological is used in some later chapters).

Chapter 2: A new Critical Discussion considers neurotransmitters and human memory.

Chapter 3: In this chapter on development, discussion of critical periods and of Freud's psychosexual stages has been deleted, while a Critical Discussion on sex differences in behavior, based on Maccoby and Jacklin, has been added. "Role diffusion" is now called "role confusion." A final section on development as a lifelong process is organized around Erikson's psychosocial stages.

Chapter 5: In this chapter on perception, the discussion of perceptual influences of needs and values has been deleted, while coverage of Neisser's analysis-by-synthesis theory has been added.

Chapter 6: This states-of-consciousness chapter has been substantially rewritten and rearranged, although most of the content remains similar to the Sixth Edition. In this edition, however, much more attention has been given to definitions and variations of consciousness, and to consciousness as an agent of control, while a Critical Discussion considers the behaviorist's rejection of consciousness. The latest findings in sleep research have been added, including discussion of narcolepsy and apnea. Discussion of meditation now contrasts TM with Herbert Benson's non-ritualized derivation, as explained in his book *The Relaxation Response.* A major addition at the end of the chapter warns students against claims of the miraculous offered without proof, for example, "psychic surgery" and reincarnation.

Chapter 7: In this chapter on learning, the section on multiple-response learning has been deleted, while the discussion of computer-assisted instruction (CAI) from the Sixth Edition's deleted Chapter 9 has been moved here; it is also now retermed *computer-assisted learning (CAL).* A Critical Discussion on punishment replaces that material from the deleted Chapter 9, while *secondary reinforcement* has been retermed *conditioned reinforcement.*

Chapter 8: This memory chapter has been totally rewritten to reflect the latest views of memory processes. It emphasizes cognitive approaches and includes such topics as constructive processes. It retains very little from the Sixth Edition, although the discussion of the key-word method for language learning, from the deleted Chapter 9, has been incorporated. See the text for other details.

Chapter 9 (formerly 10): This language chapter has also been totally rewritten and retains little of the Sixth Edition version. It includes expanded coverage of visual forms of thinking and creativity. See the text for details.

Chapter 10 (formerly 11): In this basic motivation chapter, the portion on sex has been expanded and now includes coverage of homosexuality and transsexualism.

Chapter 11 (formerly 12): In this chapter on human motivation and emotion, coverage of aggression, including the potential effects of televised violence, has been expanded. Coverage of lie detection has been made into a Critical Discussion and expanded to include the voice stress analyzer.

Chapter 12 (formerly 14): This chapter on intelligence has been moved so that it now precedes the personality chapter rather than follows it. Coverage of heritability as a concept has been expanded and the concept of reaction range added. Guilford's structure-of-intellect model has been deleted, while the discussion of convergent versus divergent thinking that was formerly part of the discussion of Guilford has been expanded as part of a new subsection on intelligence and creativity.

Chapter 13 (formerly 13): This personality chapter now follows rather than precedes the intelligence chapter. The three theoretical approaches have been resequenced so that the social learning approach is discussed second (after the trait approach), and the psychoanalytic approach third, rather than vice versa. Assessment techniques have been taken out of the separate theoretical discussions and compiled into a separate section on assessment, which also includes a new Critical Discussion on controls for faking and response style and another on the Barnum effect. The issue of consistency, formerly a Critical Discussion, is now a separate section.

Chapter 14 (formerly 15): In this conflict and stress chapter, the defense mechanisms have been resequenced, with denial added as a separate section and undoing dropped. The discussion of reactions to frustration has been somewhat trimmed down, while a major new section on stress and its effects has been added. This latter includes discussion of psychosomatic problems and the "executive monkey" studies, formerly covered in Chapter 16. It also includes a new Critical Discussion on biofeedback and another on measuring life stress.

Chapter 15 (formerly 16): This chapter on abnormal behavior now refers to *abnormality* rather than *psychopathology* and uses slightly different nomenclature, for example, *phobia* instead of *phobic reaction*. A major change is the elimination of psychophysiological disorders; as noted above, this discussion now forms part of the stress material in Chapter 14. A major addition is a section on alcoholism and drug dependence, while a new Critical Discussion alerts students to the potential changes in diagnostic categories in DSM-III.

Chapter 16 (formerly 17): In this therapy chapter, behavioral therapies are now discussed before client-centered therapy, which is treated under the new general heading of *humanistic therapies. Somatotherapies* are now more simply termed *biological therapies*, and *chemotherapy* is called simply *drug therapy*.

Chapter 17 (formerly 18): This social psychology chapter has been extensively rewritten and rearranged. Bystander intervention is retained but presented at the beginning, as an example of the social-psychological perspective. Social influence has been moved to the second section and expanded, using the Patty Hearst case as a focus for the discussion of various forms of influence, including compliance. The discussions of social perception and attribution, which have been rewritten, now conclude the chapter.

Chapter 18 (formerly 19): This psychology and society chapter has also been extensively rewritten. Only portions of the behavioral science and public policy discussions remain from the Sixth Edition and these have been reworked; a new Critical Discussion on jury selection has been added. Most of the chapter is new, with extensive coverage of prejudice, for example, including the authoritarian personality and techniques for changing prejudice. Influences of the mass media are considered, as is environmental psychology, including research on both noise and crowding.

4. Using *Introduction to Psychology*. If you use the complete text in sequence, you need only decide what, if any, of the appendix you will assign. Several variations are possible, however. The Critical Discussions, for example, are so written as to be independent of the text itself and may be omitted at your discretion; while they include interesting and controversial material, some of this coverage may be more than you wish to assign. Some of you may wish to omit entire chapters; as noted earlier, chapters are also written so as to be relatively independent of each other, making this choice feasible. Chapters may also be rearranged, for the same reason, though the introductory material in the first chapter is an important lead-in to all other chapters; therefore, the first chapter should be retained as the first reading assignment.

By selecting particular groups of chapters, you may create relatively specialized briefer courses. Two possible outlines are given in the Preface to the text, one for a course with an experimental-biological emphasis and the other for a course with a personal-social emphasis. There are, of course, many other possible outlines, some of which might call for assigning parts of chapters, asking for more extensive reading without responsibility for taking examinations on everything, or omitting the Critical Discussions.

Although the text's authors believe that all the chapters are valuable, they are willing to recommend discretionary omission for several reasons: (a) Not all colleges and universities are alike; (b) not all introductory psychology courses are alike; (c) instructors should take responsibility for designing their own courses, based in part on their own interests and background; (d) students' ultimate acquaintance with psychology need not be limited to the chapters that are assigned. They will not be deprived or shortchanged because some chapter has not been assigned:

It is there for them to read if they wish to. If they go on in psychology, they will have other opportunities to correct any deficiencies.

B. THE *STUDY GUIDE WITH PROGRAMMED UNITS AND LEARNING OBJECTIVES*

1. Goals. The *Study Guide* is intended to provide a general aid to students in mastering the course content. It attempts to help with the major problems that students tend to encounter: difficulty with the key terms and concepts of the course, lack of feedback as to how well they are doing until an exam is given, and difficulty with understanding and appreciating the role of research in psychology.

2. Structure and Features. There are five major components in the *Study Guide:* learning objectives, programmed units, terms and concepts, self-quizzes, and exercises. A complete set of these five components is provided for each chapter of the text plus the appendix.

The *learning objectives* are the important ideas from the chapter that students should master; they provide an overview of the study goals for each chapter. There are ten objectives for each chapter.

The *programmed units* are a major feature of the *Study Guide.* They attempt to cover *most* of the important concepts in each chapter, although space considerations do not allow all topics to be covered. These programmed units are intended to be used as a *preview* of the corresponding text chapters. They do not attempt to provide the finer distinctions and subtle points of the text and do not cover the Critical Discussions at all. These units help students achieve familiarity with the terms and concepts in the chapter; the chapter itself can provide the appropriate qualifications and exceptions.

The key *terms and concepts* introduced in each chapter are listed in the *Study Guide.* Most of them appear in the glossary at the back of the text, although more thorough definitions can be developed by study of the presentation in the chapters. Terms from Critical Discussions are included, but these are marked with an asterisk, so that they may be skipped if desired.

The *self-quizzes* are another major feature of the *Study Guide.* Each consists of 20 multiple-choice questions designed to be answered *after* the chapter has been read and studied. These are distributed across the material of the entire chapter, with at least one question for each of the ten learning objectives. An answer key is provided at the end of each self-quiz; it includes a page reference from which the question was taken. The questions in the self-quizzes may overlap those in the Test Item File in subject matter, but the presentation is never identical. This overlap is intentional; without it the self-quizzes would define for the students what would *not* be on the exams. The self-quiz questions are often somewhat longer and more difficult than the average question in the Test Item File; thus, they aid study of the material, as well as test it, but do not include any questions on the Critical Discussions.

The final section in each chapter of the *Study Guide* is one or more *exercises* or demonstrations intended to illustrate important concepts from the text chapter. Most of them are designed to be carried out by students individually, though for some of them several students may combine data; a few of these exercises, however, must be conducted by the instructor.

3. Differences from the Sixth Edition. All major components of the *Study Guide* are similar to those of the Sixth Edition, but there are some differences in details. All chapters now have exactly ten learning objectives and the self-quizzes have been designed so that each objective is covered by at least one question. The terms and concepts now include some from the Critical Discussions (marked by an asterisk). The keys to the self-quizzes now include text page numbers for reference. An increased number of the exercises are intended to achieve student interest and involvement rather than to be re-creations of psychological experiments, although many of the latter type are still included.

4. Using the *Study Guide*. From your point of view, the major question is whether to use a study guide at all. But you then have to choose between the *Study Guide* and the *Mastery Study Guide* described in Section IVC below. One possible compromise is to order a limited number for students to use on an optional—that is, "recommended" rather than "required"—basis, if you do not intend to formally use either guide. (Past experience shows that many students will buy and use one of these guides on their own under such circumstances and are usually quite glad to have it.)

Whether or not you require that students use the *Study Guide*, you should remember to review the exercises therein for possible lecture or demonstration use.

From the students' point of view, the *Study Guide* components offer different kinds of aids, to suit different problems and to be used in different ways. The list of learning objectives should be examined first, last, and at intervals in between, for it summarizes the important points to be understood; as students gain in understanding, these objectives will have increasing meaning.

As noted earlier, the programmed unit should be worked through before the corresponding chapter is read. If used as intended, it will substantially improve the students' mastery of the text. (The psychological rationale for programmed instruction is discussed in Chapter 7 of *Introduction to Psychology.*)

Students should read the list of terms and concepts before they work on the chapter, but formal completion of these should be attempted only after they study the chapter. This list defines specific and concrete knowledge to be achieved and thus complements the list of learning objectives.

Students should attempt the self-quiz only after they have read and studied the chapter. This is intended to offer students an opportunity to realistically assess their mastery of the material—and warn them if it is inadequate—before the real exams are given. In the process, it also will serve as a review of important points in the chapter.

The exercises are intended to aid in understanding the material and may be done whenever appropriate; however, they are likely to provide maximum aid if students have read through the chapter beforehand.

C. THE *MASTERY STUDY GUIDE* AND THE *MASTERY INSTRUCTOR'S GUIDE*

1. Goals. The *Mastery Study Guide* and the *Mastery Instructor's Guide* are basically intended to provide the framework for a "unit-mastery" or "Keller plan" course format, as described in Section IIB10. They are so designed, however, that they may also be used within the format of a conventionally structured course.

2. Structure and Features. There are four major components in the *Mastery Study Guide*, which correspond in general to four of the five components of the *Study Guide with Programmed Units and Learning Objectives* but differ in content and arrangement. These consist of learning objectives, terms and concepts, study questions, and practice quizzes. How they correspond to the components of the *Study Guide* is discussed below; the exercises found in the *Study Guide* have no counterpart in the *Mastery Study Guide*.

The *Mastery Study Guide* is divided into units, each unit representing a text chapter or, for the more difficult and complex chapters, one-half of a text chapter. There are a total of 28 units for the 18 text chapters plus the appendix. Each unit is further subdivided according to the major subheadings of the text chapters, typically into three or four subsections.

Each subunit consists of one or more learning objectives, a list of terms and concepts, and a set of study questions. The *learning objectives* are identical to those used in the *Study Guide* and in the Test Item File. The lists of *terms and concepts* and the *study questions*, however, are more extensive and more detailed than those found in the *Study Guide*. The terms and concepts also include some major names, for example, Freud, Maslow, and Skinner, unlike those of the *Study Guide*, and the study questions are not in programmed form but are a mixture of types, including fill-in-the-blanks, matching lists, labeling diagrams, and so on. These also include periodic "hints" designed to help ensure conceptual understanding of difficult points. At the end of the unit are two alternate 10-question multiple-choice *practice quizzes*, similar in format and coverage to the mastery quizzes provided in the *Mastery Instructor's Guide*. As with the *Study Guide*, an asterisk denotes terms or study questions taken from the Critical Discussions of the text, so that these may be skipped if the instructor chooses to do so.

The *Mastery Instructor's Guide*, provided only to instructors, consists primarily of four alternate 10-question multiple-choice quizzes for each unit. These are designed to be used directly as duplication masters for copying quizzes. In addition, four alternate forms of two 25-question multiple-choice review tests are provided, with the first review covering units 1–10 and the second, units 11–20. Four alternate forms of a 50-question final exam are also included; 20 questions review units 21–28, and 30 review all prior units. These review tests and final exams are drawn from all alternate forms of the unit tests. They may be used in addition to the unit tests or could be used as midterm and final exams in a conventional course structure. (If all four alternate forms are not necessary in such a structure, two or more forms could be combined, yielding, for example, two 50-question review forms and two 100-question finals.) Answers to all questions are provided separately, together with the corresponding learning objective and text page references.

3. Differences from the Sixth Edition. For the Seventh Edition, the general format of the *Mastery Study Guide* and the *Mastery Instructor's Guide* remains the same.

4. Using the *Mastery Study Guide*. Once you have decided to use a study guide, you will have to determine which of the two available ones best suits your needs, the *Study Guide with Programmed Units and Learning Objectives* or the *Mastery Study Guide*. The latter can be used simply as a required or recommended study aid and it can also be used in a more structured mastery plan of course organization.

If you use the *Mastery Study Guide* in a mastery plan, such as those described in Section IIB10, the *Mastery Instructor's Guide* includes the alternate forms of achievement tests for such a plan. If, however, you do not use a mastery plan, then the *Mastery Study Guide* may still suit your needs. As described in Section IVC2, the *Mastery Study Guide* offers more comprehensive and more detailed questions than the *Study Guide*, and these are designed to serve as a framework for detailed study rather than as a programmed introduction to the text chapters. Since it does not include the exercises in the *Study Guide*, however, you will thus have to decide which is more appropriate for your course. (Note that if the *Mastery Study Guide* is used, you can draw on the exercises in the *Study Guide* as further lecture or demonstration aids.)

If you do use the *Mastery Study Guide* in a non-mastery course structure, remember that you can either create your own exams from questions in the Test Item File (described in Section IVD) or use the midterm and final exams included in the *Mastery Instructor's Guide* (described in Section IVC2).

D. THE TEST ITEM FILE

1. Goals. The Test Item File is intended to provide you with multiple-choice questions that cover the important points of each chapter. The questions require understanding of the material rather than pure rote memorization, to as great an extent as feasible, and vary in level of difficulty.

2. Structure and Features. The Seventh Edition Test Item File includes 100 multiple-choice questions per chapter (including the appendix), plus specially identified items covering the Critical Discussions. The entire set of questions is provided at once, rather than in annual series. The Test Item File comes in two formats: As in the past, it appears in printed form and is now also available on computer tape (both described further below).

Each page of the printed form of the Test Item File is printed with six questions, perforated, so that the items can be separated into 3 X 5 cards and filed. Each card includes the chapter, topic, text page from which the question is taken, corresponding learning objective, and space for recording use of the question and percentage passing. In addition, each includes the word *Knowledge* or *Understanding*. This is designed to indicate the emphasis of each item, although of course there is no hard-and-fast distinction between the two categories.

The computer format, containing all the questions of the printed Test Item File, is available on 9-track, 1600 BPI and 9-track, 800 BPI tape, which can be converted to 7-track tape, if needed. The tape will produce a print-out that duplicates the organization of the printed format: The questions are arranged according to chapter and numbered within each chapter. The resulting print-out also includes the chapter number, the question number, the corresponding learning objective, and the answer for each item. The identifying code to the right of each item also identifies the question as testing for knowledge or understanding, as does the printed format.

3. Differences from the Sixth Edition. The Seventh Edition features several innovations in the test program. First, the Test Item File has been greatly expanded. In the past, three annual series of the Test Item File were provided. Each series contained 20 multiple-choice questions, plus additional items for the Critical Discussions. As noted in Section IVD2, the Test Item File now contains 100 multiple-choice items per chapter plus Critical Discussion items, and the entire set is issued at once. Second, the emphasis of each item is indicated by the word *Knowledge* or *Understanding*, as discussed in IVD2. Another major innovation is the availability of the entire Test Item File on computer tape as well as in the printed form.

4. Using the Test Item File. If you use the printed format, you will probably wish to cut up the pages into separate cards and file them in sequence. Numbered index file dividers are available from stationers for separating the cards by chapter. You may also add your own questions to this file by typing them on 3 × 5 cards and inserting them in sequence (by page number).

With the computer format, the identifying code to the right of each item on the print-out enables you to access the questions for making up tests—either specific questions or a random sampling. If you want to produce print-outs in class-sized quantity for tests, you will need to program the computer to skip the first line of each item, since it includes the answer.

In making up tests, you will probably want to decide first how much emphasis each chapter will receive in terms of numbers of questions. You can then select from the available set the ones that you want, based on the points you feel are important and how difficult you wish your questions to be. Regardless of the general level of difficulty, you will probably want some relatively easy and some relatively hard questions; the easier questions allow the less capable students to demonstrate some knowledge and provide success experiences for the others, whereas the harder questions help to sort out the most competent students.

An important aid in making good tests is a file of locally tested examination items. When an item has been used with a sample of reasonable size, calculation of the percentage passing the item will give an indication of how difficult it is. A simple rule of thumb is that best results are obtained with items averaging in difficulty halfway between the percentage expected by chance and 100 percent. Thus, in a four-response multiple-choice question, the percentage passing to be aimed for is halfway between 25 percent and 100 percent, or 62.5 percent. It is better to have questions judged too easy rather than too difficult by the criterion of percentage passing because this reduces the number of complaints about ambiguous alternatives. It is not necessary to compute the correlation of an item with the test as a whole because this tends to weight too heavily the ability (intelligence) component of test-answering. If the face validity of the item is satisfactory for measuring what is being taught, then the percentage passing is a preferred measure.

Once items have been selected, you need to make up the actual exams. You want to end up with duplicated question sets, answer sheets, a scoring key, and an annotated copy of the exam, one with both correct answer and page reference for each question. The annotated exam is important. It allows you to check the text reference in answering student questions, both during the exam and afterward. You might even wish to make the annotated copy available to students immediately after the exam, for feedback.

In making up the exam from the printed format, you can save much effort and time by using duplication equipment. The question cards are arranged so that they can be overlapped to make up an exam, using two columns on 8½ × 11 paper turned 90°. The best plan is to xerox each page of overlapped cards (masking the information on the top card with a blank one). Page numbers and question numbers can then be typed on this xerox copy to make a master; once this is available, any of a variety of duplication systems can reproduce the exams in bulk.

There are several ways of holding the cards for the initial xeroxing. You can simply arrange them in clear plastic folders, but they tend to slump out of position when the folder is moved. Small pieces of Scotch Magic Tape will hold them, and will not interfere with the xerox, but the tape is troublesome to remove. Or you can prepare a sheet of light cardboard—half of a manila folder is fine—with a series of diagonal cuts so that the top corners of the cards can be inserted. If this is then placed in a clear plastic folder of the type used for term paper covers, the cards will stay in place for xeroxing, yet can be easily removed and refiled without damage to them. Remember that you want an annotated copy, however, and plan accordingly. If you wait until your cards are taped together or removed and refiled before trying to develop a set of answers and page references, it will add substantial and unnecessary effort.

If your school uses any form of computer grading, you will, of course, arrange your answer sheets accordingly. If you or someone helping you must hand-score the exams, however, you may wish to use a system such as the following, which allows reasonably quick scoring and can provide an estimate of question difficulty without any computation.

The basic idea is simply to arrange your answering system so that a grading stencil can be laid over the students' answer sheets and incorrect answers noted. One way to do this is to arrange the answer sheet with the answers, ABCD, in a row after each question number and instruct students to mark the desired answer with an X directly through it. You can then make one or more scoring stencils by punching holes, corresponding to the correct answers, in one of the answer sheets. When this grading stencil is laid over a student's answer sheet, correct answers will show X's in the stencil holes. If no X shows, a diagonal red mark in the hole both marks the question wrong and gives the student the correct answer. A problem with this system is changed answers. For changes, students should obliterate the original answer entirely, then X the new choice. An obliterated answer in the stencil hole is thus also wrong. (However, some who change will want to change back and will write margin notes to that effect, so whoever scores the exams will want to check for such notes when an obliterated answer appears.)

If you wish to get some indication of question difficulty without computation, simply begin and end your red mark on the stencil sheet itself. By varying the angle of the mark as necessary, you can build up a pattern around the stencil holes. The most difficult questions will eventually be surrounded by solid red; the easiest will show only a few marks. If the number of papers is not too large and you are extraordinarily neat and precise in grading, you can even count the marks and thus obtain the percentage correct, but it is probably best to simply note the very easy and very hard questions for future reference.

With the printed format, multiple-choice questions can also be used as the basis for other kinds of questions. They can be turned into true-or-false questions by typing the question and one of the available answers, for example. (Each multiple-choice question thus offers four possible true-false questions.) Furthermore, some of the multiple-choice questions can be easily adapted to short-answer questions by typing only the question and letting students supply the answer. Others, in which a single term or short identification is to be matched to another, can become identification questions if used alone, or can be used jointly to provide a "match column A to column B" question, with several questions used for column A and some or all of the multiple-choice answers listed in column B. (Remember, also, that Section VI of this handbook provides short-essay questions.)

E. THE FILMS

1. **Goals.** Each of the series of films available from Harcourt Brace Jovanovich, Inc., has been designed to provide in-depth treatment of a major topic in contemporary psychology. Each conveys the major psychological principles, findings, methods, and interpretations, using real psychologists in each field as consultants, narrators, and participants. As a series, the films provide a general supplement to the text, re-

lated closely enough to provide easy integration with text material, yet different enough to supplement the text rather than repeat it.

2. Structure and Features. All five films in the series were produced by a leading documentary film maker, Lee R. Bobker, of Vision Associates, Inc. Each is in color and is approximately 25 minutes long. (Exact times are noted below.) Three of the five films feature a single-well known psychologist; the others draw on the work of several such psychologists. (Further details of each film are given below, following the description of service policies.)

All films may be rented or purchased, with current users of the text offered a 50 percent discount on either rental or purchase. Rental films are booked for a three-day period; weekly rentals may be arranged for double the regular rate. Films are shipped via parcel post special handling, or United Parcel Service, insured, and must be returned in the same manner. Previews are available with intent to purchase only; these may be booked for three-day use, free of charge, except for return postage and insurance. A rental fee may be applied to the purchase price, should you decide to buy within 60 days of rental. Should you decide to keep and purchase the same print you receive as a rental print, you will receive a further 10 percent discount off the purchase price.

The films available include:

Child's Play: Window on Development
Sandra Scarr (Yale University)
Consultant and Narrator

Child's Play is a lively introduction to the aims, methods, and perspectives of the developmental psychologist. Through a wide variety of scenes of children at play—ranging from the exploratory play of a six-month-old infant with a new toy to the relatively complex forms of reasoning exhibited by an adolescent playing a board game—the film shows how children work out and practice their relations with others and with their world and how they acquire increasingly complex perceptions about themselves. The various forms of play—dramatic, sensory, skill-mastery, and social play—serve as major socializing and learning experiences. People of all ages reveal their cognitive and social levels through play, and the psychologist can use this sort of naturally occurring behavior as an excellent means for studying development from infancy to adulthood. 20 min. Color. 1976.

When Will People Help? The Social Psychology of Bystander Intervention
Daryl J. Bem (Cornell University)
Consultant and Narrator

In this film, social psychologist Daryl Bem uses bystander intervention as an example of the kind of problem with which social psychologists deal. After introducing the topic through a brief discussion of the Kitty Genovese murder, the film presents reenactments of several important experiments that illustrate how social psychologists test their hypotheses. It explores the reasons for bystander nonintervention, shows how laboratory and field experiments have led to a reasonable explanation for the social phenomenon of nonintervention, and suggests ways of overcoming bystander nonintervention and getting people to help another person in distress or in an emergency situation. The material in the film relates directly to Bem's discussion of bystander intervention on pages 520–23 of the textbook. 25 min. Color. 1976.

Divided Brain and Consciousness

With Ernest R. Hilgard (Stanford University), Jane Mackworth (Santa Clara Valley Medical Center), Robert E. Ornstein (The Langley Porter Neuropsychiatric Institute), and Elliot S. Valenstein (University of Michigan)

This film introduces students to the research and findings on the functioning of the cerebral hemispheres. The four major segments of the film present some of the tests developed by Jane and Norman Mackworth to study brain-damaged patients; demonstrations by Ornstein of experiments that use an electroencephalograph to record the alpha rhythm of brain waves in normal subjects; reenactments of some of the tests developed for use with split-brain patients; and Hilgard's use of hypnosis to demonstrate what he calls "divided consciousness" and the phenomenon of the "hidden observer" (which is also discussed in depth on pages 180–82 of the textbook). The four types of experiment shown in the film—along with Valenstein's interpretive remarks—offer students a graphic demonstration of the functions of the right and left hemispheres of the brain and also acquaint students with a variety of techniques psychologists use to study the human brain and consciousness. 22 min. Color. 1977.

Human Memory

Gordon H. Bower (Stanford University)
Consultant and Narrator

Human Memory explains and illustrates the aspects of memory, memory aids, and the cognitive distortions created by constructive memory processes. The first segment demonstrates what it is like to have no memory at all. The film then establishes the difference between short-term memory and long-term memory, with brief demonstrations illustrating the limited capacity of short-term memory. It then shows how real learning involves the transfer of information from short-term memory to long-term memory and illustrates several learning methods. Further demonstrations illustrate how the use of more effective retrieval cues can improve one's ability to remember. Finally, an experiment using a rumor chain illustrates the cognitive distortions that are produced when individuals reconstruct memories. The film's demonstrations and discussions reinforce the conclusion that memory is the key to our ability to learn and one of the most important and distinguishing faculties human beings possess. 28 min. Color. 1978.

The Psychology of Eating
Elliot S. Valenstein (University of Michigan)
Consultant and Narrator

The Psychology of Eating looks at such questions as What motivates animals and humans to seek food? Why do we choose some foods and avoid others? Why do some people become obese? and What are some strategies for losing weight? The film begins with the studies of Lewis P. Lipsitt of Brown University, which indicate that even newborns have strong taste preferences and that experience affects taste preference at an early point in life. The next sequence illustrates how John Garcia of U.C.L.A. has modified animal behavior by using aversive conditioning to certain tastes. In other studies, Terry Powley of Yale University shows that animals do respond to an internal signal that reflects their need for food but that animals that cannot taste food consume less and weigh less than animals that can. The fourth sequence presents some of Valenstein's research, which focuses on the capacity of animals to control their own body weight by regulating the amount they eat, and on the role of the hypothalamus in the process. Judith Rodin of Yale University then demonstrates her studies on the responsiveness of obese and normal weight individuals to external stimuli such as the sight and smell of food. Finally, Albert J. Stunkard of the University of Pennsylvania discusses his study and treatment of obesity, especially his use of behavioral analysis in helping people achieve weight control. The film thus concludes by linking basic science—psychology and physiology—with clinical practice in the study of how and why people eat and how that behavior may be changed. 29 min. Color. 1978.

3. Using the Films. A general discussion on the use of films in the introductory course is provided in Section IIB6, and details for the use of these films and others are presented in the chapter-by-chapter discussions in Section VI.

V. EVALUATING THE COURSE/INSTRUCTOR

A. EVALUATION PURPOSES

1. For the Students. Student evaluation of the course and instructor can be beneficial to the students making the evaluation as well as to future students.

For current students, the opportunity to evaluate can involve them in their own and other students' education and can help them to view the course, instructor, and even psychology more favorably. This assumes, of course, that they perceive the school's and/or instructor's motives as furthering the improvement of the course and not simply as a "con." Presuming that the school and instructor are, in fact, seeking improvement, the use of student input can also help students who take revised versions of the course. If evaluations are made before the end of the semester, it may be possible to modify some aspects of the current course, offering students even more direct involvement. (If this is planned in advance, the syllabus may be left open-ended toward the end of the course.)

If information about course/instructor evaluation is available to would-be students, it can be useful in choosing courses. Such evaluations can be provided formally, within the school's structured system, or in more or less accepted ways outside it—for example, openly distributed "confidential reports" written by students or surreptitious information of one sort or another.

Another student "purpose" that may also be served, however—unfortunately in some respects—is the release of hostility. Regardless of the source of students' hostility or the accuracy of students' perception of its source, the opportunity to anonymously evaluate the system often results in a few students venting their hostility on the course, and often on the instructor personally. Clearly, this is not a desirable educational purpose, however cathartic or therapeutic it may be for the students. Its probable occurrence must be recognized, however, in the analysis of such evaluations.

2. For the Instructor. The most educationally relevant function of student evaluation for you as an instructor is as feedback. It is one thing to assess how the course is going, or how it went when it is over, strictly from the podium and red-pencil side; it is quite another to assess it from the audience and test-taking side. The differences can be highly illuminating and can offer valuable inputs to improving your teaching. The potential improvement in student morale and/or motivation is also valuable.

3. For the School. In one sense, anything that helps students or faculty helps the school; thus, the purposes listed above are also those of the school. Those purposes specifically for the benefit of the school, however, are the evaluation of the (student-perceived) quality of a particular instructor, a particular course, or both. While not likely to be taken as sole criteria for establishing the quality of either course or instructor, student evaluations can be used as a major input in decisions regarding both.

From the school's viewpoint, such evaluations also allow broader comparisons: one instructor versus another, one introductory course versus another, one department or even division versus another, or changes over time. As such, they can be part of the data used in decisions about students' transferring, choosing majors, etc. In this regard, they serve the same function for the school overall as they do for a particular instructor: They say what the students think about their education. As more standard forms become available, it may even begin to be possible to compare the results from different schools—certainly those within a single system such as a large state system. If this happens, evaluations may come to have the influence over the performance ranking and budget decisions regarding schools that they are beginning to have over instructors' ratings.

Some critical voices have been raised, however. Professor Leon W. Zelby, of the University of Oklahoma, for example, writing in *Science*, warns of the dangers of teaching for maximizing evaluations—"mediocrity of education," in his view. Zelby also feels that widespread use of such systems would tend to widen the gap between first-rate and second-rate institutions, in that the selected student populations of the former will praise challenging education while those of the latter will favor mediocrity. (For further discussion of these problems, see Zelby's article "Student-Faculty Evaluation," *Science* 183 (1974): 1267–70.)

B. EVALUATION SYSTEMS

1. During the Course. Most formal evaluation systems described (for example, McKeachie, Appendix B, as listed at the end of Section I) are based on evaluations given at the end of a course. In effect, they ask "How did it go?" By using numerous techniques it is also possible to obtain "real time" evaluations during the course —that is, to ask "How is it going?" Some structured ways of teaching the course— for example, mastery systems such as the Keller plan (described in Section IIB10)— provide such information. And to some extent the examinations in a conventional course (especially if essay questions are included) provide information on student progress. But our concern here is with systems for specifically obtaining course evaluation.

One system calls for the use of short evaluation sheets for particular course units, such as exams or movies; this allows changes to be made in later exams and permits students to evaluate events immediately after their occurrence rather than at the end of the semester.

This could be expanded to a more extensive ongoing evaluation system. One such method used by the author involved "feedback sections"; two of the sections within a topic-discussion system had as their topic the introductory course itself. These sections met with the instructor rather than with a TA, thus providing a two-way channel of communication between instructor and students. An attempt was made to create a nonthreatening atmosphere and to involve the students in improving their own and future students' education. The students discussed questions posed by the instructor, raised questions or made suggestions of their own. They informally polled friends outside of the section meeting and, at the end of the semester, wrote papers summarizing their views of the course and possible improvements. This method allowed the instructor to keep track of student opinion in real time and to incorporate useful student suggestions within the same course from which those suggestions came, as well as in later courses. At the same time, it informed students about some of the compromises necessary in teaching such a course, the reasons for objective testing, and so on, while providing the powerful motivational appeal of allowing them a voice—albeit only by suggestions—in their own education. While no guarantee is offered, all parties concerned seemed to benefit from the experience, and it is submitted as one possible way of keeping in touch with the class. (The students were volunteers for these sections and thus not a representative sample, but the bias was in favor of conscientious and concerned students who were able to provide valuable feedback.)

A less formal feedback system is simply to encourage students to tell you how it's going; this system, however, usually provides biased and less useful information than that gained from a feedback section. Students are understandably reluctant to come to you with either praise or criticism, lest they be seen as buttering you up or risk their grade, respectively. Furthermore, students who do overcome this inhibition (a) *may* be trying to butter you up, if their comments are favorable; (b) are likely to have overcome the criticism inhibition only because they are worried and distraught or perhaps naturally critical, if their comments are unfavorable. These are biased samples, often troublesome to deal with effectively, and yield questionable information. While you may wish for other, more humanitarian reasons to leave your door open to students with problems, it is not likely to be a very useful source of feedback information.

In addition, any other people involved in the course can provide feedback to you. You can ask other faculty members to sit in on your class and evaluate it, or just to report what they have heard informally from students. TAs can be valuable sources of feedback, as can others in a position to pick up student comments—for example, your department secretary.

A final suggestion is to evaluate yourself. Many schools now have videotape equipment; sometimes this is specifically available for such evaluative purposes; in other cases it might be possible to arrange to borrow it. (If it is available, it can also be used to aid your TAs in evaluating their teaching.)

2. At the End of the Course. Most evaluation systems now in use are given at or near the end of a course. They are not intended to directly influence the current course but to evaluate it and its instructor so as to enable future decisions to be made. Numerous systems are in use, several of which have been published. (See sources noted below.) A single system may be used, with the resulting data used for two or more different functions—for example, for instructors to be able to improve and for the school to decide if it will keep them in the meantime. Or two or more separate systems may be used—for example, one for the school, and perhaps instructor, and a different one for the students.

Such systems may be required, voluntary, or mixed—for example, the school's forms required and the students' forms voluntary. The only truly voluntary forms are probably those you make up yourself, however; if formal systems already exist, there will be pressure to use them. If you feel they will be supportive of your teaching, by all means use them. You may even wish to bring your self-created ones to the school's attention if the results are good. On the other hand, if you are unsure of the results, you will simply have to decide which stands to hurt you least: possibly poor evaluation results or refusing to evaluate. If you do face such a decision, you might be wise to evaluate during the course, as suggested in the previous section. At least that way you have some knowledge of what the final evaluations may be expected to show.

If you plan to make up your own system, you may wish to consult what others have done. Individual professors or committees at a number of schools have developed local forms, some of which are available to schools. These include, for example, one created by Professor James B. Maas, of Cornell University, which includes a manual of instructions. Single copies are available from Dr. Maas (115 Rand Hall, Cornell University, Ithaca, N.Y. 14850); multiple copies can be obtained from Cornell (stock item #G18255, Cornell General Stores, Cornell University, Ithaca, N.Y. 14850). A computer program for statistical analysis of the results is also available from Cornell's Office of Computer Services (Ithaca, N.Y. 14850). Professor Wilbert J. McKeachie, of the University of Michigan, has also published a form (Appendix B in his book listed at the end of Section I). But be careful. There are very many pitfalls in developing such a form; a change in wording can drastically change results, and a form that works for one class format may not for another. And there is always a problem of norms. If your numbers look good, how good are they really?

For these and other reasons, an increasing number of schools are using the SIR form (for Student Instructional Report) offered by Educational Testing Service (Princeton, N.J. 08540). It is professionally developed, offers optional questions for you to ask about your particular class, and can be compared to a number of systems of norms that their computer can generate: for your school as well as similar ones nationally, for class size and type, and so on. Unless your school has a carefully designed and tested local form, this is probably the best system to use.

3. Analyzing the Evaluations. The purpose of this section is not to tell you how to do statistical analysis but to suggest how to keep your equilibrium in a procedure very likely—almost certain—to involve and punish you emotionally.

In a sense, your position with respect to evaluation is a twist on the students' position in grading. The students who get A's typically deserve them and fully expect them, and hence they are not terribly rewarding. Many other students who had expected or at least hoped to get A's do not, however, and this *is* very *non*-rewarding. For you, who presumably work hard and believe in yourself, good evaluations are satisfying, but, after all, deserved. The not-so-hot evaluations, on the other hand, are definitely disturbing, and the few "blasts" that are almost certain to be included can be devastating to a delicate ego. Those experienced instructors reading this section may chuckle, perhaps with a faintly remembered twinge of anxiety. But for new instructors, severe anonymous criticism by students can be very distressing.

Several things kept in mind when analyzing the results will help you retain an objective and analytical perspective. First, remember that the broad heterogeneity of the students you are likely to have typically renders everything a compromise. The *best* you can expect on a question that asks if the work load was appropriate, the course broad or narrow enough, and so on, is a normal distribution about the ideal answer. If about the same number of students criticize you for a too narrow course as do so for one too broad, you must have balanced it well.

If you wish to analyze further, you may be able to correlate answers with other variables, such as class. If you have a class that is mostly freshmen and have oriented to them, do not be surprised if senior students (from other fields, taking introductory psychology as a filler) criticize you for talking to them as if they were freshmen.

A few supercritical evaluations are to be expected and should not be taken too seriously. They often come from the poorer students (as indicated by errors of spelling and syntax) who may be taking their frustrations out on you. The time to pay attention is when the overall numbers come out where you wish they hadn't or when a large number of students make similar spontaneous criticisms. These results are more likely to be valid. While such evaluations will be disturbing, it is probably better to discover your faults now—if you plan to continue teaching—so that you can correct them.

You should keep in mind, however, that unless you have baselines, you don't really know what constitutes a good performance. In order to know how well you did, you need not only numbers for the whole school, but also those for division, department, and, ideally, the same course as taught by others. Lacking the latter, you may be able to get data for similar large introductory courses. (As noted earlier, the ability to provide such comparative data is a major advantage of the SIR form offered by Educational Testing Service.)

If you continue to teach the same course, your own previous numbers are of course your best baseline for personal growth. You may be assured from experience, if this is to be your first term, that you can and will get better, and both you and students will recognize the improvement. So if your numbers aren't really very good the first time, just think of how large a gain is possible.

VI. CHAPTER-BY-CHAPTER TEACHING SUPPLEMENTS

This section of the handbook provides, for each chapter, a very brief reminder of the content of the chapter, suggested films, suggested lecture topics and/or demonstrations, and short-essay questions. Remember, with respect to lectures and demonstrations, that the *Study Guide* offers group exercises for many chapters. These are noted in Section IVB; see the *Study Guide* for details. A film supplier is listed for each film; addresses for these suppliers are included in the list given in Section IIC5. Details of films available from Harcourt Brace Jovanovich, Inc., are provided in Section IVE. The abbreviations used in this section are listed below.

CRM	CRM/McGraw-Hill Films
EMC	Extension Media Center, University of California
HBJ	Harcourt Brace Jovanovich, Inc.
HM	Houghton Mifflin Co.
MH	McGraw-Hill Films (not available from CRM)
PCR	Psychological Cinema Register, Pennsylvania State University
PH	Prentice-Hall, Inc.
HR	Harper & Row Media

While a few films are available only from particular suppliers, many of the others are available from several sources, especially the other large university collections noted in Section IIC5.

When a film is appropriate for more than one chapter, it is described in the most appropriate one; parenthetical references in the other chapters note where the description may be found.

CHAPTER 1: THE NATURE OF PSYCHOLOGY

Summary

Chapter 1 presents five basic approaches to psychological issues to be used throughout the text, with a Critical Discussion of developmental and interactive explanations of behavior. It notes the subfields of contemporary psychology—experimental, developmental, and so on—and the methods of psychology, including experimental design and basic statistics.

Chapter 1 Film Suggestions

Aspects of Behavior. CRM. An overview of contemporary psychology. Interviews with noted psychologists and descriptions of their experiments, including Darley and Latané's famous "smoke-filled room," demonstrations of electrodes implanted in the brains of rats and Delgado's bull to control their behavior, schizophrenia discussed by psychologists with divergent views, and the late Abraham Maslow's last filmed interview. 31 min. Color. 1971.

Methodology: The Psychologist and the Experiment. CRM. An informative visual account of how research experiments scientifically test hypotheses. Animation and special effects help show the common features of all research, including independent and dependent variables, control groups, random assignment, and so forth. Uses as examples two different experiments: Stanley Schachter's fear and affiliation study and Austin Riesen's study of kittens' visual-motor coordination. Winner of several awards. 31 min. Color. 1975.

(*Research in Animal Behavior*; see Chapter 10.)

Scientific Method in Action. EMC. Galileo's work introduces the scientific method as a way of conducting an experiment in order to solve a problem. Authentic footage shows Jonas Salk and his research team utilizing Galileo's approach in their discovery of vaccine for infantile paralysis. 19 min. Color. 1960.

Chapter 1 Lecture/Demonstration Suggestions

A key to understanding psychology is to understand the different theoretical approaches and methods of psychology. You will probably have to put special emphasis on the scientific method itself and on the intent as well as the techniques of psychological experimentation. The meaning of a correlation (and that it does *not* define causation) and of a level of significance is also important. These are all in the text but will need to be emphasized.

A way to present the nature of the problems involved is to contrast "grandmother knowledge"—the things your grandmother knew were true—with scientific psychology. You can use well-known folk sayings to illustrate that this "knowledge" can be completely contradictory and not at all helpful in *prediction*. For example, is it "Absence makes the heart grow fonder" or "Out of sight, out of mind"? Is it "He who hesitates is lost" or "Look before you leap"? This can be worked into the scientific method versus the "common sense" method, as Barry Anderson puts it. His book *The Psychology Experiment: An Introduction to the Scientific Method*, 2nd ed. (Belmont, Calif.: Brooks/Cole, 1971) is a good reference here.

You can also present exactly the opposite of the results of a study and see if everyone agrees that "their grandmother knew that," or you can use the results derived from a U.S. government study on violence by Stark and McEvoy, writing in *Psychology Today* on "Middle Class Violence" (November 1970, p. 54). They begin with a series of statements that at least some of your students might be expected to agree with—for example, "Middle-class Americans are more likely than working class persons to vent their rage in symbolic and nonphysical ways"—except that all are false, according to the study.

Yet another way of making your point is to lay out for your students the sequence of investigation: "observe-hypothesize-predict-test." With this on the board, you can discuss how it works in familiar terms. Suggest they wish to figure out why their roommate does a certain bizarre thing. (Everyone's roommate does *something* bizarre.) Then show how to do this in the steps noted, with test results supporting the hypothesis or not, and so on. You can elaborate as far as you like, suggesting how to control other variables than your hypothesized one, and so on.

As you do so, you might want to warn them of how hypothetical constructs can become circular explanations, perhaps noting the steps on the board: "as if"-hypothetical construct-"reality"-explanation. You can choose many examples—obviously psychology has at least its share of them—but the notion of "crazy" behavior is one that seems clear to them (where "crazy" begins as a *label* of bizarre behavior and quickly becomes the *cause* of it).

Other lecture points can be elaborated from material given in the text. For example, you could build more correlation-but-not-causation items around the notion of temperature-related phenomena, similar to the hot asphalt-sunstroke one used in the text.

One old but still intriguing article is John Somerville's "Umbrellaology, or, Methodology in Social Science," *Philosophy of Science* 8 (1941). It thoroughly spoofs too great a reliance on methodology without meaningful content by describing a hypothetical science of the study of umbrellas.

A somewhat similar classic warning about methodology is Huff's *How to Lie With Statistics* (New York: Norton, 1954).

Chapter 1 Short-Essay Questions

1. How would a psychologist representing each of the five major viewpoints of psychology (given in Chapter 1) approach the problem of human aggressive behavior?
2. Briefly state the history of the definition of psychology, specifically in terms of the use of the words "mental processes" and "behavior."
3. List (one, two, three, and so on) of the noted types of psychologists and describe what they do in their professional work.
4. What is meant by the behavioral or social sciences, and how does psychology fit into these?
5. Describe the basic functions of independent and dependent variables in an experimental procedure, being sure to clarify the differences between them.
6. Note (one, two, three, and so on) of the four methods for psychological investigation listed in addition to the experimental method.
7. Describe the function of a control group and specifically how it differs from an experimental group.
8. Describe the advantages and disadvantages of a multivariate experimental design as opposed to a single variable one.
9. In simple terms, what does it mean to say an experimental result is statistically "significant"?
10. When or why would one use correlational techniques in psychological investigations?

CHAPTER 2: BIOLOGICAL BASIS OF BEHAVIOR

Summary

Chapter 2 begins with the neuron and synapse as the basic units of the nervous system, with a Critical Discussion on neurotransmitters and memory. It then considers the organization of these units in the central nervous system. The hierarchical structure of the brain is discussed, with a Critical Discussion on how the brain is studied. This is followed by specific consideration of the cerebral cortex and a separate discussion of the split-brain research and its implications. Separate descriptions of the divisions of the autonomic nervous system and the endocrine system follow, with the final portion devoted to genetics.

Chapter 2 Film Suggestions

Autonomic Nervous System. EMC. Employs live action, animation, and scenes of living organs (through gastroscopy and catheterization) to show the workings of the autonomic nervous system. 17 min. Color. 1975.

Brain: Creating a Mental Elite. EMC. Examines three major areas of brain research: chemical stimulation, electrical stimulation, and environmental conditioning. Includes discussions with Wilder Penfield, Roy John, Mariam Diamond, and David Krech. Writer Arthur C. Clarke also comments on some imaginative possibilities. 22 min. Color. 1972.

Divided Brain and Consciousness. HBJ. Four major segments include Jane and Norman Mackworth showing tests for lateralized brain damage, Robert E. Ornstein demonstrating alpha brain wave conditioning, a re-creation of testing of split-brain patients, and Ernest R. Hilgard using hypnosis to demonstrate the "hidden observer." Interpretive remarks throughout by Elliot S. Valenstein. 22 min. Color. 1977.

Genetic Defects: The Broken Code. EMC. Defines genetics terms, such as "chromosomes," "genes," and "meiosis," and depicts the ways genetic diseases are passed from parents to children. Examines the principle genetic defects in the U.S., such as cystic fibrosis, Huntington's chorea, and sickle cell anemia. Describes amniocentesis and considers some of the dilemmas of genetic counseling. 90 min. Color. 1976.

Genetics: Man the Creator. EMC. Surveys current research and explores possibilities for human genetic engineering. Shows and discusses a sperm bank, an embryo transplant in a goat, and a lamb embryo growing in an artificial womb. Explains cloning, speculates on genetic surgery, and interviews a genetics counselor. Closes with a discussion of the moral issues. 22 min. Color. 1971.

The Hidden Universe: The Brain (In two parts). CRM. Provides an overview of brain functions, including motor control, memory, and perception. David Janssen as host integrates segments that include an operating room scene with brain stimulation, scenes of a young man with a "split brain," a young woman with an implanted spinal stimulator, and the attempt to develop artificial vision. A variety of brain malfunctions are also discussed, together with the drugs, techniques, and equipment currently used to diagnose and treat them. Award winner. Total: 45 min. Color. 1977.

Miracle of the Mind. MH. Reviews research being conducted into the nature of the brain and chemical and electronic means of improving its functional capabilities. Considers the theory that certain drugs can increase motivation, competitiveness, even IQ level. Notes that transfer of certain substances from one brain to another may be the forerunner of "smart pills." CBS Reports. 26 min. Color.

Nervous System in Man. EMC. Uses animation and live subjects to show how the human nervous system, together with the endocrine system, provides coordination of movement and integration of bodily functions. Explains nerve impulses, parts of the brain, central, peripheral, and autonomic nervous systems, and related topics. 18 min. Color. 1965.

Peripheral Nervous System. EMC. Employs scientific demonstrations, animation, and models to explain and illustrate the nervous system, the transmission of nerve impulses, and the relationship of reflex action to the spinal cord and brain. 19 min. Color. 1977.

(*Prenatal Development*; see Chapter 3.)

The Split Brain and Conscious Experience. HR. Michael Gazzaniga, one of the pioneers in this field, explains the split-brain phenomena, using rare and unusual footage of actual surgery and patients. 18 min. Color.

Chapter 2 Lecture/Demonstration Suggestions

This chapter is difficult for students and thus is one in which you will want to stick pretty closely to the text. Also, the sizes, shapes, and interrelations of the components involved are hard to grasp, so that films, slides, three-dimensional models, or real-tissue samples can be very useful. (See the preceding section for film suggestions and Section IIC5 for slides.)

It is particularly useful to be able to show what the brain looks like and how it relates to other structures. For the brain itself, it is psychologically powerful to be able to show a real human brain. If your school has a medical school, you may be able to borrow one (preferably sectioned, or at least split to show the corpus callosum).

It is less messy and more permanent, however, to use models. A plastic model of the brain and upper spine is available, but you might as well go on to show the relationship of the brain and spine to the skull by obtaining the complete kit called "The Visible Head." This life-size model has a clear plastic molded "head," through which the muscles and bones can be seen when fully assembled. It can be substantially disassembled to show the inner components: The outer head splits and comes off, the skull top lifts off, the hemispheres lift out and split, the cerebellum lifts out, and portions of the skull lift out to show the inner ear. The kit comes with a very comprehensive illustrated booklet and is stocked by most large suppliers of plastic models (or presumably could be obtained from the manufacturer, Renwal Products, Inc., Mineola, N.Y. 11501).

Chapter 2 Short-Essay Questions

1. Describe a nueron, noting the major components and their general function in nerve impulse transmission.
2. Describe the electrochemical process of propagation of a nerve impulse along a single neuron (and across a synapse).
3. Describe, and note the differences between, the "central" and "peripheral" nervous systems.
4. Note the minimum three components of a simple reflex and how they work together to form the reflex.
5. Name and describe (the three, the innermost of the three, the middle one of the three, or the outermost of the three) concentric layers of the human brain. (This yields four possible variants of the question.)
6. Name and describe the functions of (one of the, two of the, three of the, four of the, the five) major types of human cortical areas. (This yields five possible variants.)
7. Describe the separate functions of the two hemispheres of the human brain, as researchers now view them.
8. Name and compare the functions of the two parts of the autonomic nervous system.
9. Describe the general functions of an "endocrine gland" and name one of the two most important ones.
10. Describe the relationship between genetic and environmental influences on behavior, including one or more examples.

CHAPTER 3: PSYCHOLOGICAL DEVELOPMENT

Summary

Chapter 3 begins with the factors governing development—maturation and experience—and their interactions. It discusses Piaget's cognitive development stages, with a Critical Discussion of moral stages, then considers issues of personality development in early childhood, with a Critical Discussion on child care for working mothers. It then discusses the process of identification, with a Critical Discussion on sex differences in behavior, and concludes with the role of the adolescent, the search for identity, and development as a lifelong process.

Chapter 3 Film Suggestions

Adolescence: The Winds of Change. HR. John J. Conger presents and discusses the problems of adolescent development. The physical, sexual, and cognitive changes of adolescence and the effects of parental attitudes are discussed, both by adolescents and by Conger, plus David Elkind and Jerome Kagan. 30 min. Color.

Aging. CRM. Two major sociological theories describing the relationship between the aged individual and society are discussed; an exploration of California's "Leisure World" illustrates the "activity theory," and an urban locale is the setting for a look at the "disengagement theory." A series of personal interviews with aged individuals illustrates some of the more common and successful psychological patterns of aging. Award winner. 20 min. Color. 1973.

(*Battered Child*; see Chapter 10.)

The Child Series. CRM. This National Film Board Series is a departure from the usual CRM format. It offers strictly documentary cinéma vérité recording of the normal family and growth patterns of seven infants, which can be most effectively used to illustrate lecture or text points. Each, 28 or 29 min. Color.
   The Child: Part I; The First Two Months. 1975.
   The Child: Part II; 2–14 Months. 1975.
   The Child: Part III; 12–24 Months. 1975.
   The Child: Part IV; Three-Year Olds. 1978.

The Child Watchers. MH. Uses unrehearsed situations to point up some of the new techniques psychologists are using to measure early child development. Produced by Time/Life Broadcast, Inc. 30 min. Color.

(*Children's Aggression: Its Origin and Control*; see Chapter 11.)

Child's Play. CRM. Shows how mental, social, emotional, and physical growth are linked to a child's form of play and how these forms change as the child grows older. 20 min. Color. 1978.

Child's Play: Window on Development. HBJ. Narrated by Sandra Scarr, it provides a graphic introduction to the aims, methods, and perspectives of the developmental psychologist. A wide variety of scenes of children at play—from a six-month-old infant with a new toy to an adolescent with a board game—are used to show how children work out and practice their relations with others and with their world, and how they acquire increasingly complex perceptions about themselves. 20 min. Color. 1976.

Cognition. HR. The development of perception, memory, evaluation, and reasoning for American children from birth through adolescence. Includes descriptions of Piaget's stages. One of a series written by Jerome Kagan and Howard Gardner. Award winner. 30 min. Color.

Cognitive Development. CRM. Piaget's stages are contrasted with behaviorist theory and practices. Animation and special effects depict the child's growth. A visit to a Piagetian school reveals a freewheeling "creative" atmosphere, while a visit to a behaviorist school finds psychologists drilling children with specific, programmed data. Suggests that both views have given us valuable insights. 20 min. Color. 1973.

A Cross-Cultural Approach to the Acquisition of Sex Roles and Social Standards. HR. Three different cultural settings—Kenya, Guatemala, and Japan—illustrate the similarities and/or differences in social standards that are the result of modernization, economic status, and degree of isolation. Children are shown learning by observation, imitation, praise, and punishment. In-depth analysis is made of identification with "ego-ideal." Of special interest are the differences in acquired sex-role standards. One of a series edited by Jerome Kagan. 25 min. Color.

A Cross-Cultural Approach to Cognition. HR. The same cultures as above, but with a focus on the invariant sequence of milestones in psychological development. Task-oriented experiments show how modernization of the environment can affect the rate of emergence of these milestones. Winner of several awards. 22 min. Color.

Development. CRM. A journey from birth through adolescence, with many stops along the way to visit prominent psychologists and discuss their views of a variety of aspects of development. Concludes with a discussion of what adolescence is and how society should react to youthful ferment. 32 min. Color. 1971.

Development of the Adult. HR. Explores the "ages and stages" of the adult years, with filmed interviews with Bernice Neugarten, Roger Gould, Daniel Levinson, Paul Costa, and David Gutmann. They present their views as the film looks at the complex interplay of forces that shape our adult years. Includes coverage of such questions as whether adult crises are normal or predictable, whether men and women differ in adulthood, and how culture affects our adult development. 25 min. Color.

(*Emotional Development: Aggression*; see Chapter 11.)

Everybody Rides the Carousel. EMC. Superbly animated rendering of Erik Erikson's eight stages of personality development. Uses brief, universally understandable

103

vignettes to illustrate the principal developmental challenges and crises of each stage as well as to symbolize the primary conflicting forces in the personality. Top awards. 72 min. Color. 1976.

From Cradle to Classroom (In two parts). MH. Modern educational programs are attempting to start the education of children as early as 12 months. Special teaching machines and instructional techniques increase not only physical skills such as locomotion, but motivational, verbal, and conceptualizing abilities. Educational toys and association drills at the earlier ages, and reading and logic practice for the 2-, 3-, and 4-year-old group are explained and demonstrated, as are the controversies that early-age education causes. CBS Reports. Total: 52 min. Color.

Growing Old: Something to Live For. CRM. An upbeat look at older citizens and the gap between the way they see themselves and the way the rest of the population views them, produced by ABC News. In three segments, covers general attitudes toward growing old, working versus retiring, and the development of special housing. Includes interviews with the late Margaret Mead, Gray Panther Lydia Bragger and other active, working older people who demonstrate what lively and useful members of society they can be if allowed to be. 15 min. Color. 1978.

Growth Failure and Maternal Deprivation. EMC. Clinical study showing that physical and mental retardation in young children may often result from a lack of parental attention, especially from the mother. Demonstrates clinical features of infantile marasmus in two girls from fatherless homes and impoverished surroundings. Given "massive doses of tender loving care" as well as medical treatment, both show dramatic improvement. 28 min. Black and white. 1967.

(*Individual Differences*; see Chapter 13.)

Infancy. CRM. Shows babies at different ages in an experimental setting and in natural home environments exploring and discovering the real world, learning the nature and permanence of objects. 20 min. Color. 1973.

Infancy. HR. Discusses behavioral and cognitive patterns characteristic of infancy, such as object permanence, stranger and separation anxiety, reaction to discrepancy, and maturing of coordination. Also shows individual differences in temperament. One of a series written by Jerome Kagan and Howard Gardner. Winner of several awards. 21 min. Color.

(*Language Development*; see Chapter 9.)

(*Moral Development*; see Chapter 17.)

Moral Judgment and Reasoning. CRM. Describes the characteristics of moral development from three perspectives: psychoanalytic theory, social learning theory, and cognitive developmental theory, with emphasis on Piaget. A variety of vignettes illustrate stages of moral development and reasoning. David Rosenhan also describes Lawrence Kohlberg's work. 17 min. Color. 1978.

Personality: Adolescence. CRM. Discusses development of self-esteem, a desire for independence, and an awareness of sexual maturation as factors in teenage personality development. Uses short realistic vignettes to illustrate the themes, interspersed with comments by Barbara Newman. 21 min. Color. 1978.

Personality: Early Childhood. CRM. Describes and illustrates four aspects of the preschool personality: dependency, identification, aggression, and anxiety. Paul Mussen discusses emotional and instrumental dependency. Robert Liebert explains identification and modeling, with a replication of Albert Bandura's aggression experiment and consideration of televised and family aggression. 20 min. Color. 1978.

Personality: Middle Childhood. CRM. Describes the transition from home to peers and society in the six-to-twelve-year-old. Describes the particular influences of peer groups. Stresses the family environment as one in which motivation to achieve can be developed. 19 min. Color. 1978.

Physical Development. CRM. Provides an overview of normal physical growth and development from infancy to adolescence, including puberty. Compares perceptual and motor-skills development in early and middle childhood and shows special movement education to reduce tension and improve perceptual motor skills. 21 min. Color. 1978.

Prenatal Development. CRM. Live footage traces the formation and development of the human embryo/fetus. Examples of prenatal environmental influences are interspersed throughout the development sequence; these include the mother's diet and use of drugs, plus other factors. 23 min. Color. 1974.

The Preschool Experience: Four Programs. CRM. Discusses the programs and goals of four different preschools: an Assistance League Nursery, a Montessori School, the Gesell Nursery School in Connecticut, and Kedren Health Center in central Los Angeles. 22 min. Color. 1978.

Rearing Kibbutz Babies. EMC. Observes infant rearing in an Israeli kibbutz, organized around the weekday activities of a young mother and *metapelet* (care-taker), who cares for four infants in the Baby House and takes scheduled breaks to visit her own children in the nearby Children's Houses. Includes commentary by an American-born kibbutz mother. 29 min. Color. 1975.

Rock-A-Bye Baby. EMC. Produced by Harry Harlow. Wide-ranging examination of current research on the psychological and physical effects of early child care, including mother-deprived human infants in institutions as well as animal experiments, including Harlow's. An emotional experience as well as a thorough compilation of research data. Highest awards. 30 min. Color. 1971.

Sex Role Development. CRM. Examines the development and daily influence on our lives of sex roles and stereotypes, plus the ways in which some people are trying to find better models for human behavior. Discusses the influence of the media, toys, peer behavior, and adult expectation. Includes two examples of nontraditional sex-role socialization, one of them the daily routine of a three-year-old boy at Pacific Oaks School in Pasadena, Calif. 23 min. Color. 1974.

Three Cognitive Skills: Middle Childhood. CRM. Discusses reading, memory, and creativity as keys to normal growth. Considers their development from ages six to twelve, and the variety of factors—including individual intelligence plus school and home environment—that affect their development. 20 min. Color. 1978.

Tim: His Sensory-Motor Development. HR. Covers the period from birth to two years of age, structured around a series of tasks drawn from Piaget. Provides a look at the long-term development of a single child, showing the sequence of sensory-motor development, the interaction of cognition and affect, and the elaboration of social behaviors. 31 min. Color.

What Do You Think? EMC. Demonstrates three major stages of cognitive growth in children four- to eleven-years old. David Elkind leads a discussion with several children in which they reveal their concepts of the physical world, as well as their religious and moral ideas. Narrator explains how concepts expressed exemplify the different stages. 34 min. Color. 1971.

Chapter 3 Lecture/Demonstration Suggestions

Chapter 3 is probably not too difficult for students to absorb on their own. Thus, you may wish to add material here in addition to that of the text, especially if you have a relatively sophisticated group of students and can count on their learning the basics. As noted above, a large number of films are available, including the film *Child's Play*, specifically designed to complement the text. These could be used instead of lecturing.

Or, in presenting the chapter contents you may want to emphasize the need for each child to create the world anew. In doing so, you can look ahead to the chapters on sensation and perception, states of awareness, learning, language, personality, and perhaps even abnormal behavior; each will be relevant to the child's building a world for him or herself.

You may also wish to emphasize particular portions of the chapter because of your personal structuring of the course or personal interest. You could expand on the "nature-nurture" issue, Piaget's stages, or identification theories, for example.

Depending on your school's orientation to such things, including whether other courses exist to cover it, you could expand on the sexual development portion—looking ahead to Chapter 10. If you are covering the chapters in sequence, you will have in Chapters 2 and 3, physiology and developmental psychology, the keys to expanding on sexual development from biological and early learning perspectives. If you do, you may wish to refer to some of the numerous publications now being created for sexual education classes, such as the widely used Stanford text by Katchadourian and Lunde, *Fundamentals of Human Sexuality* (New York: Holt, Rinehart & Winston, 1973). Also of interest are Money's *Sex Errors of the Body* and Money and Erhardt's *Man and Woman, Boy and Girl* (Baltimore: Johns Hopkins Press, 1968 and 1972, respectively). While primarily oriented to sexual development problems and counseling for them, these present a useful conceptual framework of crucial sexual developmental stages, from genetics to gender role.

You may instead wish to expand on the concept of development as a lifelong process and include more material on problems of mid-life and aging, the "male menopause," and so on. In doing so, you may wish to discuss problems of longitudinal versus cross-sectional methodology in studying such questions (possibly including reference to the Chapter 12 material on assessing intelligence trends with age).

A discussion of aging would lead into the topics of death and dying. The material of Chapter 2 provides the basis for a discussion of brain death, while other sociological-psychological aspects could be expanded here, either as a part of a general coverage of aging or separately.

Yet another approach you may wish to use is to consider ethological perspectives in more detail than Chapter 3 does. Chapter 10 discusses such issues, but you may wish to consider them here, presenting possible species-specific mechanisms as inputs to the development sequence; you can easily tie this into the discussion of maturation and stages in Chapter 3.

In any case, you will probably wish to relate this chapter to the later ones in some way, reminding students that the issues are interlocked and that developmental processes will be involved in the other categories to come—for example, perception and personality.

Chapter 3 Short-Essay Questions

1. Describe the interaction of maturation and environment in a child's development and illustrate with one or more examples.
2. Briefly describe (one of the, two of the, three of the, the) four stages of

Piaget's theory of intellectual development. (This provides several possible questions; others could be formed by requesting a description of one or more specific stages.)

3. Briefly describe (one of the, two of the, the) three major levels of moral reasoning proposed by Kohlberg.
4. Compare the fundamental problems or issues in development on which Piaget and Kohlberg based their stage theories.
5. Compare the concepts of secure attachment and anxious attachment, including how you would measure them and what might cause them.
6. Discuss the following statement, including whether you agree or disagree and why: "Identification with parents and modeling of their behavior is of importance only in sex-typed behaviors."
7. Describe some of the variables that facilitate a child's identification with an adult.
8. One of the children in a family of several children is likely to be especially different from the others. Note which one and discuss why and in what ways this child is likely to differ.
9. Discuss the identity problems faced by adolescents and compare them with those of older age groups.
10. Discuss why you might consider the generation gap to be less of a gap in reality than it is sometimes said to be.

CHAPTER 4: SENSORY PROCESSES

Summary

Chapter 4 begins the discussion of the senses with a consideration of thresholds, including a Critical Discussion of ROC curves. It separately considers vision and audition at some length, with Critical Discussions on theories of color vision and hearing, then concludes with lesser coverage of smell, taste, the skin sensations, kinesthesis, and the equilibratory senses.

Chapter 4 Film Suggestions

Ears and Hearing. EMC. Shows structure and function of human ear. Demonstrates conversion of sound waves to perception. Discusses two forms of deafness and their treatment. Shows actual ear examination, using cut-away model and detailed drawings for clarity. 22 min. Black and white. Second edition. 1969.

Eyes and Seeing. EMC. Provides an understanding of the eye and its component structures, and examines some problems involved in determining how the brain evaluates and acts on visual information. Macro- and microphotography with superimposed symbols identify the parts of the human eye. Experiments demonstrate eye nerve impulses. 20 min. Color. 1968.

Eyes and Vision. EMC. Explains structure and function of human eye and complicated mechanisms of human vision. Shows how retinal image is inverted, how lens changes shape to focus images, and how pupils regulate the entering light. 10 min. Black and white. 1963.

Senses and Perception: Links to the Outside World. EMC. Describes the structure and function of the human sensory system, with specialized organs to detect physical, chemical, and mechanical stimuli. Compares these to the more highly developed sense organs of some animals. Emphasizes the structure of its eye and its complex interaction with the brain, using animation to illustrate the functions of the cornea, retina, cones, and rods. Clear introduction to a complex subject, with numerous visual examples. 18 min. Color. 1975.

Senses of Man. EMC. Shows, using animation, how various stimuli are converted into nerve impulses by body's sense receptors and discusses receptors that monitor internal organs. Discusses touch, pain, temperature, and pressure sensors, and, in greater detail, those of vision, taste, smell, hearing, and equilibrium. 18 min. Color. 1965.

The Sensory World. CRM. Uses dramatic animation demonstrating how messages travel from eyes, ears, skin, and proprioceptive systems to the brain and return to the point of stimulus. Jerome Lettvin tells why his experiments prove that the eye is part of the brain. Wilder Penfield demonstrates electrical stimulation of memory. Also includes masking, colorblindness, and the way that we construct our image of the world. Concludes with a startling display of illusions. 33 min. Color. 1971.

Skin as a Sense Organ. EMC. Clear, comprehensive, well-illustrated introduction to the varieties of receptors in the skin. Thorough, point-by-point approach; British production. 12 min. Color. 1975.

Chapter 4 Lecture/Demonstration Suggestions

The material in Chapter 4 is complex but necessary. You will probably wish to stay close to the text in lecturing, rather than adding other topics. Demonstrations are highly useful here, however, and you may wish your "lecture" to be, in fact, strongly biased toward films, slides, models, and demonstrations. In choosing them you will need to consider, among other factors, the relative ease with which your students will be able to absorb the text material. If they can do it easily, you can go on to more sophisticated treatments. If they are likely to have difficulty, you may wish to review the material, or even to concentrate on basics.

CRM's film *The Sensory World* is strongly recommended here, as it presents the eye and ear in graphic animated detail and illustrates many other points made in the chapter—colorblindness types, afterimages, and so on. Other films listed above may also be useful, as may the slide sets edited by Maas. (See Section IIC5.) Time/Life Inc. also offers a set of six color filmstrips with taped accompaniment on "Survival and the Senses." (Time/Life Multimedia, P.O. Box 644 Paramus, N.J. 07652.) Demonstrations from the text itself and from the *Study Guide* may also be done in class, in the same forms or related ones.

In lecturing, you will want to be sure that your students understand the difference between sensation and perception and perhaps provide some illustrative examples as bridges between the two chapters; for example, the visual image of an object is a visual *sensation* of it, whereas the notion of it as an object, under varying conditions, is a *perception* of it. You may also refer to Chapter 3's development and to later chapters by reminding them of the infant creating its own world. The example of colorblind persons not knowing they are colorblind, presented in the text, is one that may help to point out the idiosyncracies involved in this and the next chapter. (You might also mention the problems of the *perception* of a person born blind and by an operation suddenly allowed to see.)

Some additional material of interest that you may wish to note is the current use of information about the senses to develop artificial components of them. Such research includes the wiring of "visual" pattern information directly to the visual cortex ("Artificial Vision for the Blind: Electrical Stimulation of Visual Cortex Offers Hope for a Functional Prosthesis," *Science* 183 (1974): 440–44) and the similar wiring of "audio" information directly to the cochlea (as reported in *Newsweek*, April 1, 1974, p. 50). These developments are summarized, along with others, including a prosthetic arm controlled by neuromuscular signals, in two articles: M. Pines, "Bioengineers Reinvent Human Anatomy with Spare Parts," *Smithsonian*, Nov. 1978, p. 57, and D. Teresi, "The Real Bionic Man," *Omni*, Nov. 1978, pp. 44 +.

Chapter 4 Short-Essay Questions

1. What is the difference between an absolute and a difference threshold? Give examples of how you would measure each, for a sensory system of your choice.
2. Describe, in order, the components of the eye through which a ray of light must pass before it is coded into a neural message.
3. What are the major differences between the rods and cones of the eye—for

example, in relative numbers of each, location, differences in sensitivity, dark adaptation?

4. Why are the rules of color mixture different for mixing colored lights than they are for mixing colored pigments?
5. What are the differences between the crucial assumption of the Young-Helmholtz and Hering theories of color vision? What does the research evidence to date imply about these theories?
6. What is recurrent inhibition in a visual system and what advantage(s) does it provide for an organism that has it?
7. Describe, in order, the components of the ear through which a sound wave must pass before it is coded into a neural message.
8. What are the two current theories of pitch discrimination and how do they differ? What does the research evidence to date imply about these theories?
9. What components make up the sense of touch, and what structures in the skin give rise to them? How do these structures or the resulting components produce the sensation of "hot"?
10. What are the two specialized senses that allow us to control the movement of our limbs, and what are the sense organs that give rise to them?

CHAPTER 5: PERCEPTION

Summary

Chapter 5 considers classical perceptual issues, beginning with the perceptual constancies and including a Critical Discussion on adapting to visual distortion. It then considers the organization of perception, followed by perceptual hypotheses, movement and depth perception, and pattern recognition, with a Critical Discussion on pattern recognition models. It concludes with discussions of the roles of learning and attention and the question of extrasensory perception, including a Critical Discussion on the issues of evaluating extrasensory perception.

Chapter 5 Film Suggestions

Maurits Escher: Painter of Fantasies. EMC. Introduction to the work of the renowned Dutch artist whose works combine strict mathematical principles and perceptual illusions with sure artistic sense. Discusses his stylistic development and artistic philosophy. He describes several of his works as the camera pans over them. Objective, nonopinionated commentary. 27 min. Color. 1968.

Motion Perception (In two parts). HM. Part of a set of widely acclaimed films by James B. Maas, designed to demonstrate phenomena and stimulate thinking. Part I gives two-dimensional cues; part II gives three-dimensional cues. Part I, 7 min.; part II, 11 min. Color. 1971.

Perception. PH. Provides many principles of perception not readily available for classroom demonstration. A complete overview of the field, including definitions of sensation and perception and experiments/demonstrations on figure-ground, phi phenomenon, perceptual set, color mixture, trapezoidal window, and so on. 15 min. Color.

(*The Sensory World*; see Chapter 4.)

Chapter 5 Lecture/Demonstration Suggestions

The material of Chapter 5 offers a wealth of possible lecture/demonstration topics. Numerous audiovisual aids are available from a variety of sources, including CRM's film *The Sensory World*, already mentioned in Chapter 4, and the slide series noted in Section IIC5. Ames rooms and other pieces of demonstration equipment are available from the equipment suppliers listed in the APA's Red Book and excerpted in Section IIC6.

A source of materials that can be used to illustrate a number of visual phenomena is the work of M. C. Escher. Students are fascinated with his work—reproductions sell well at poster shops—and his manipulation of depth cues to create impossible perspectives is superb. (One of his engravings is included in the text, on page 141.) They are not likely to know, however, the extent to which his work not only demonstrates, but was derived from, research in the psychology of perception. This relationship is summarized in M. L. Teuber, "Sources of Ambiguity in the Prints of Maurits C. Escher," *Scientific American*, July 1974, pp. 90–104, while the beautifully illustrated book by B. Ernst, *The Magic Mirror of M. C. Escher* (New York: Random House, 1976) presents the finished products as well as the carefully planned preliminary drawings and perceptual analyses that led to their creation.

An extremely useful piece of demonstration apparatus that you may have to make, or have made for you, is a pair of distorting goggles. They can be created with apparatus used by optometrists to test eyes: an adjustable frame and two rotating angular-correction lenses. Glue the two plastic lens assemblies into the frames with the adjust knobs projecting to the sides. You can then rotate the lenses while a subject is wearing them, to quickly shift the vision angle. Since the optic field of such lenses is narrow and subjects can see around the lenses, the best effect is obtained when a masking goggle is worn over the distorting glasses. Obtain an inexpensive pair of molded clear plastic safety goggles of the type contoured to wear over glasses. Spray them with flat black enamel on the inside and cut out eye holes just large enough for the field of view of the distorting goggles. Another possibility is to make these out of welder's goggles. See E. T. Benjamin, Jr.'s article "Perceptual Demonstrations—Or What to Do with an Equipment Budget of $75," *Teaching of Psychology*, 3 (February 1976): 37–39.

To effectively demonstrate the plasticity of visual perception, use your glasses and goggle set as follows: Get a couple of volunteer students. Put the glasses and goggles on one, with the lateral distortion set at zero degrees. Let the subject then demonstrate that the apparatus itself does not interfere (substantially) with the ability to perform simple tasks requiring visual-motor coordination: reaching out to touch a raised hand of the other subject, reaching up to place an X in the center of a tic-tac-toe box on the board, or tossing a soft "ball" to the other subject. (Use a "ball" made of a tied-up cloth or a sock stuffed with rags, to avoid injury or damage in the procedure to follow.) Subjects should be able to do this, even though their vision is displaced vertically.

Then have the subject close his or her eyes and adjust the glasses to maximum lateral distortion; use either direction but be sure that both lenses are adjusted in the same direction. When the subject again tries the same simple tasks, the effects should be quite spectacular. The first throw or reach will be off by the amount of distortion of the lenses you have—perhaps 20° to 40°. Within a few tries, however, the subject will be able to correct—though not without some effort and difficulty. When the throw is corrected, have the subject close his or her eyes and reverse the polarity of the distortion. This time the "correction" will be added to the distortion and the first effort should be approximately twice as far off as before. Let the subject again correct, perhaps while he or she comments on the accompanying sensations. (The subjective effects of trying to recorrect the kinesthetic feedback are interesting—as if you were pushing the arm into a dense substance, or were having an external force pull it to one side.)

Finally, when the subject is well adapted, have him or her try the task without the goggles. Typically, subjects expect everything to be normal as soon as the goggles are off. In fact, they do recover quickly but still show the effects of the last adaptation for one or two trials. This residual distortion in the absence of the apparatus, and thus obviously a product of the subject's own visual-motor coordination, can be one of the most impressive aspects of the demonstration if it works. (If the subject recovers so quickly that it isn't obvious, you might praise him or her for the ability to do so and point out that not everyone recovers so quickly.)

If you wish to spend the time, discuss the strategies that subjects are using for correction, then control some of these strategies and note the differences in result. One strategy for ball tossing, for example, is to simply toss the ball to the side of your receiver, knowing intellectually that it will reach him or her. This does not yield the kind of adaptation you want. Instead, the subject should concentrate on the receiver, look directly at him or her (as seen through the glasses), and concentrate on throwing straight at the receiver. This takes longer to correct, but yields the subjective sensations noted earlier and the overshoot when the distortion is reversed. One adaptation is intellectual; the other is visual-motor.

Be sure students understand that it is the kinesthetic sense of the arm that adjusts to fit the vision. This helps demonstrate the importance of vision for human beings, compared to the other senses. (To emphasize this point you might note that the sound from a TV or film seems to come from the appropriate visual source—even though our hearing is easily able to directionally pinpoint the source in the absence of the visual cues.) To demonstrate that the change is kinesthetic, have an adapted subject try the other hand. Even if one hand is well adapted, the other must begin essentially from zero.

Another very effective demonstration, if the equipment is available, is speech disruption by delayed auditory feedback. The effects are powerful, virtually impossible to prevent, and can be started and stopped with the flick of a switch if the apparatus is set to do so. The equipment works by recording the speech of the subject and simultaneously playing it back. If the subject hears, via earphones, only the playback, the time for the tape to move from the record head to the playback head introduces a delay that is very disruptive of speech. This works to some extent with a conventional recorder, but the best effects, as well as the range in type of disruption, can be obtained only when the distance between the heads can be easily varied and when the audio to the subject can be conveniently switched back and forth between delay and real time. Specially designed recorders are available for this purpose.

Inverting glasses can also be useful, though somewhat less dramatic than the lateral-distortion ones. A simple, though not very effective, set can be made from a pair of the plastic goggles suggested above for covering the lateral-distortion glasses. Paint the insides flat black as before and cut a slit across the full width above the normal vision line; glue a mirror on the outside, just above the slit and projecting forward several inches. If the angles are appropriate, a subject will be able to look through the slit and see in the mirror an inverted image of objects directly ahead. This view is very limited in scope, and it is very hard for the subject to use it to move around much.

You can use it to demonstrate disruption of writing, however, which can be usefully related to either of the previously described demonstrations. If a subject with inverted vision is simply asked to write his or her name on the board, while looking at it carefully, few can get beyond the first couple of letters before tangling hopelessly. If instructed to do so, however, the subject can simply ignore the visual input, even though still looking at it, and write his or her name on muscular patterns only. Point out that, after all, you can do a credible job of signing your name in the dark. It is not the lack of appropriate feedback that causes the prob-

114

lem; it is the conflict between correct kinesthetic cues and inappropriate visual ones. In this case, the performance is so overlearned it can be done by "disengaging" the visual cues cognitively. (About the only way to minimize the disruption in the delayed auditory-feedback procedure is via a similar strategy, but this is far less effective in overcoming disruption.)

All of these demonstrations can be integrated via the concept of feedback and sensory-motor coordination patterns. All are effective; they are interesting to students and are well remembered.

Luria's *Mind of a Mnemonist* (New York: Avon Books, 1968) provides a useful and interesting discussion of the phenomenon of synesthesia. You might pose the question of whether anyone might be able to see sounds or smell them, and what sounds might look or smell like. A discussion of Luria's case should allow you to bring out aspects of normal sensory integration and interaction, as well as the possibilities of unusual forms such as Luria describes.

A final suggestion for a demonstration is based on the auditory phenomenon similar to the visual one of the disappearance of a stabilized image. If a single word is repeated *exactly*, over and over, the recognition of it "saturates" and the word is heard as something else. "Cogitate," for example, may become "agitate"—or even "fornicate." The effect is striking and happens whether or not you know what to expect. Note that the repeat should be exact, for maximum effect. To do this, tape record the word once and then duplicate that version enough to establish a tape loop that you can play.

This demonstration shows quite effectively (1) the tendency of the nervous system to function only with stimulus change and (2) the "hypothesis-testing" nature of perception.

Chapter 5 Short-Essay Questions

1. Describe the various perceptual constancies and how they combine to yield apparently constant objects.
2. What is a figure-ground relationship, and why is it of interest to psychologists?
3. How can an "object" be considered to be a "hypothesis," and what does a Necker cube tell us about this issue?
4. What are some of the known factors and remaining problems involved in the perception of movement?
5. Discuss the monocular and binocular cues that enable us to perceive depth.
6. Discuss the types of feature detectors known and how their hierarchical arrangement operates in the perception of objects.
7. State the nativist and empiricist positions on perception, with research evidence supporting each view.

8. What are some of the cues that we can use in selectively attending to one spoken message among several? What factors make this task more difficult?
9. Discuss the orienting reflex—what it is, why it might have evolved, and how one can examine it in the laboratory.
10. Discuss some of the reasons why many psychologists find ESP experiments unconvincing.

CHAPTER 6: CONSCIOUSNESS AND CONTROL

Summary

Chapter 6 begins with a discussion of consciousness and several variations thereof, including nonconscious, preconscious, and unconscious processes, with a Critical Discussion on the behaviorist's rejection of consciousness. Divided consciousness is considered, ranging from attention shifts to multiple personalities. Sleep and dreams are then discussed, including a Critical Discussion on the effects of REM deprivation. Meditation is considered, with TM followed by Benson's nonmystical derivation. The effects of psychoactive drugs are discussed, followed by hypnosis, including a Critical Discussion on controversies over hypnosis. A final section warns students to separate what is, or may be, possible from fraudulent claims of miraculous events, such as reincarnation.

Chapter 6 Film Suggestions

Alcoholism: A Model of Drug Dependency. CRM. The use of alcohol can lead to acquired tolerance, addiction, and withdrawal symptoms, just as with any other drug. This film gives both the basis and implications of that finding, including the progression of intoxication, as well as genetic, personality, and learning theories. An animated sequence explains the way our bodies break down alcohol. 20 min. Color. 1972.

Biochemical Revolution: Moods of the Future. EMC. Examines increasing development and use of mood-influencing drugs. Notes that despite the $135 million spent per year on drug education, students detect a credibility gap. Speculates on drugs for social control and stimulation of memory and intelligence. Advocates realistic approach to drug abuse, on the assumption that drug-taking is a permanent aspect of North American culture. 22 min. Color. 1971.

(*Divided Brain and Consciousness*; see Chapter 2.)

Drink, Drank, Drunk. EMC. Provides advice for those with alcoholic spouses and friends, using name entertainers such as Carol Burnett, and a varied and entertaining format. Suggests how to recognize and deal effectively with the alcoholic and describes Al-Anon, an organization for the families of alcoholics who refuse treatment. 59 min. Color. 1974.

Mind of Man. EMC. Documents worldwide studies on mind functions, including control of "involuntary" processes, development of mind in the fetus, drugs, sleep and dreams, and brain structure. 119 min. Color. 1971.

(*Miracle of the Mind*; see Chapter 2.)

Perfect Drug Film. EMC. Relaxed and colloquial history of drug use and the search for the nonexistent perfect drug. Considers the history as well as the personal and social effects of numerous psychoactive drugs. Describes what the properties would be of the perfect drug but warns that the escapism still inherent in its use would reflect a lack of self-respect and social conscience. 31 min. Color. 1972.

Sleep and Dreaming in Humans. HM. Part of a set of widely acclaimed films by James B. Maas, of Cornell, designed to demonstrate phenomena and stimulate thinking. Shows the procedures used for recording all-night sleep and dreaming behavior (with William Dement of Stanford). 14 min. Color. 1971.

The Sleeping Brain. HM. Part of the same set as *Sleep and Dreaming in Humans* (above). Demonstrates techniques for ascertaining the structures and functions of sleep and dreaming mechanisms (with M. Jouvet). 23 min. Color. 1971.

What Time Is Your Body? EMC. Explains and demonstrates circadian rhythms and how the body's internal clocks affect mood and activity. Shows results of experiments where subjects are isolated from time cues. Shows how to measure these rhythms and how to use them in preventive health programs. Stresses the importance of body harmony and includes such data as the time of day when sex hormones are most active. Top award winner. 24 min. Color. 1967.

Chapter 6 Lecture/Demonstration Suggestions

The film *Divided Brain and Consciousness*, referenced above, was specifically designed to complement the text, primarily this chapter. One aspect of the film worth elaborating on (or using even without the film) is the possible implication of the split-brain research, described in Chapter 2, with respect to consciousness phenomena. If you have not already considered such issues, see the book by Robert Ornstein (who is seen in the film), *The Psychology of Consciousness*, 2nd ed. (New York: Harcourt Brace Jovanovich, 1977), in which he speculates on them at some length, or his article "The Split and the Whole Brain," *Human Nature*, May 1978, pp. 76-83.

Much of the material in Chapter 6 is of great interest and immediate concern to students. All have slept and dreamed, and many have experienced altered states of consciousness via one or more psychological or chemical techniques. This provides motivation, which can help you, but also makes it possible that some students may know more about some aspects of the material than you do. It is probably best to pick for elaboration the one area of those covered in Chapter 6 that interests you most and with which you feel most comfortable.

It is perfectly possible to do a demonstration in class of a meditation technique, or of a hypnotic technique, but such procedures should be used only if you are knowledgeable and the school is likely to be accepting. (A consideration in planning any unusual activity in the classroom is whether it will cause trouble.)

One overall approach to states of consciousness that you may find useful is to consider them in terms of the mind/body problem, contrasting the cognitive and neurobiological approaches. Consciousness itself can be described in either cognitive or neurological terms, and as consciousness varies, it presumably does so in both terms. A particular "state" of consciousness is then least conceptually susceptible to description and specification in two languages: a cognitive or subjective one and a neurological one. Some of the parameters we can currently state, if not exactly specify—for example, "sense of time," or "activity level in the reticular formation" —whereas others remain quite unknown. An "altered" state of consciousness then becomes a change large enough to be worth noting, in one or more of these parameters, with respect to some base level or range.

You can also note that extreme reliance on only one of these approaches is likely to yield biased answers. You might suggest—if you agree that it is true—that some doctors today are too oriented toward a "physical" approach to the body, drawing too easy analogies to machinery—assuming, for example, that a deep anesthetic turns off consciousness, when, in fact, patients have been able to remember, with certain techniques, what was said during their operations. You might also point out—if you agree that it is true—that Christian Scientists place excessive reliance on the subjective experience of the world and too little on the physical reality. You may wish to use different examples, but the point seems worth making: Both an experiential or cognitive, and a mechanistic or neurobiological description may be "true," at the same time, yet total reliance on either can be misleading.

To point out to your students the difficulty in defining altered states of consciousness when our "normal" consciousness varies so widely, you might ask them, rhetorically, if they would like to have access to an altered state of consciousness that is free, easily available, nonaddictive, not only legal but socially encouraged, helpful to the body, and offers the possibility of any experience imaginable—to fly, to create, to enjoy unbounded sexual pleasure, and so on. Of course, they would—but only a few will recognize your description of dreaming. You can then point out how altered a state from waking dreaming is and how young children must learn to differentiate it from reality. As adults we fail to recognize how altered a state it is because of our familiarity with it. (Recent developments in sleep research are summarized in J. Fincher's "Sleepers are Given Polygraph Tests to Solve a Riddle," *Smithsonian*, November 1978, pp. 85–95.)

A good source of articles for debunking popular nonsense, whether cloaked in the garb of pseudoscience or not, is the journal *The Skeptical Inquirer* (formerly *The Zetetic*), developed by a prestigious group of scientists for the express purpose of publishing such articles. One current fad, for example, that gains much of its influence from the existence of real biological rhythms as discussed in this chapter, is the phony concept of charted "biorhythms." W. S. Bainbridge deals with this in "Biorhythms: Evaluating a Pseudoscience," *The Skeptical Inquirer*, Spring/Summer 1978, pp. 40–56, in which he includes a manipulation of students' biorhythms akin to the "Barnum effect" discussed in Chapter 13 (p. 404).

Chapter 6 Short-Essay Questions

1. Distinguish between nonconscious, preconscious, and unconscious processes.
2. Explain what is meant by a multiple personality and how this condition may be related to our own divisions of consciousness.
3. Describe the sequence of sleep stages that a person goes through in the first hour and a half of sleep.
4. What was Freud's theory of dreaming, and what have been some of the theoretical and experimental criticisms of it?
5. What are some of the major questions asked by researchers about the nature of dreams, and what answers have been obtained so far?
6. Describe Benson's technique of relaxation and explain how it is both similar to, and different from, the procedure used in TM.
7. Compare the effects on the user of (two of the, three of the, four of the, five of the, the) six major psychoactive drugs noted in the text to be causing major social concern. (This provides five possible question variations.)
8. Note and describe the six characteristics of the hypnotized state in a highly susceptible individual.
9. Describe some of the phenomena of hypnosis and discuss how the concept of the "hidden observer" has been applied to them.
10. Explain the differences between such phenomena as biofeedback and firewalking, on the one hand, and psychic surgery or Uri Geller's starting of watches, on the other.

CHAPTER 7: CONDITIONING AND LEARNING

Summary

Chapter 7 begins with discussion of classical conditioning, including a Critical Discussion on theoretical interpretations thereof. Aspects of operant conditioning are then covered, including a Critical Discussion of reinforcement schedules. The principle of reinforcement is treated separately, including brain stimulation and a Critical Discussion on punishment. Cognitive learning follows, including insight, latent learning, and a Critical Discussion on cognitive maps. The final section considers the individualization of learning through computer-assisted learning (CAL).

Chapter 7 Film Suggestions

Behavior Modification in the Classroom. EMC. Shows the use of operant conditioning and modeling procedures to increase children's task orientation, including successful application in three different classroom situations—early, intermediate, and older primary school grade levels. Demonstrates the need for determining appropriate rewards and generalizing reward from objects to verbal and nonverbal reinforcement. Also details methods for training teachers by role modeling, and defines the role of school psychologist in introducing and evaluating behavior modification methods. 24 min. Color. 1970.

(*Behavior Modification: Teaching Language to Psychotic Children*; see Chapter 16.)

Behavior Theory in Practice (Parts I–IV). PCR.
Part I: Introduction, respondent behavior, basic terms, selection of a response for basic research, the cumulative record, operant conditioning, extinction.
Part II: Schedules of reinforcement (fixed and variable), shaping various operants, various species, programmed instruction.
Part III: Generalization, discrimination, measurement of sensory capacities, discriminative stimuli and the control of behavior. Motivation, reinforcement, punishment, avoidance, intracranial self-stimulation.
Part IV: Sequences of behavior, homogeneous chains, heterogeneous chains, alternative responses, multiple-stimulus control.
Each part: 20 min. Color. 1966.

B. F. Skinner and Behavior Change. EMC. Sympathetic portrait of Skinner; shows him in his lab, addressing a student audience, talking with colleagues. Stresses the value of positive reinforcement practices. Raises some critics' arguments but gives them little attention. 42 min. Color. 1975.

Business, Behaviorism and the Bottom Line. CRM. B. F. Skinner explains how the "tools" of scheduling, shaping, and positive reinforcement can be used in business and industry. Shows his program in action at Emery Air Freight; they saved $2 million over three years through this performance improvement system based on accurate feedback and positive reinforcement. 23 min. Color. 1972.

Classical and Instrumental Conditioning. HR. Written and narrated by Howard Rachlin. Compares both forms of conditioning through the use of live laboratory footage interwoven with graphics. Demonstrates how these principles also apply to human beings, including a sequence that involves the audience in a dramatic experiment in classical conditioning. 20 min. Color. 1978.

Complex Behavior: Chaining. PCR. Demonstrates chaining behavior by a rat in a complex apparatus involving a spiral staircase, a drawbridge, a ladder, a cable car, another ladder, pressing a piano key, a tunnel, and a descent in an elevator to obtain food reinforcement. Shows the application of principles of food deprivation, stimulus control, and differential reinforcement in order to shape the response. 7 min. Black and white. 1969.

A Conversation with B. F. Skinner. CRM. Skinner answers some of his most persistent critics and covers the origin of behaviorism and its basic principles, the notion of control, with its use and potential misuse, punishment and freedom, the resistance to a behavioral technology, and the hidden controls of our culture. He also discusses some of the problems involved in implementing behavior modification systems and concludes with a discussion on the survival of a culture and the definition of humans. 23 min. Color. 1972.

Learning. CRM. Uses split-screen, animation, live action, and silent-screen techniques to handle a wide range of material. Opens with a spoof on species-specific behavior, then presents important experiments on the role of sign stimuli in behavior, imprinting, infant learning, and behavior shaping—including operant conditioning used in teaching language to a mentally retarded child. B. F. Skinner and D. C. McClelland narrate the closing sequence dealing with human dignity, motivation training, and the power of rewards. Winner of several awards. 30 min. Color. 1971.

Observational Learning. HR. Written and narrated by Robert Liebert. The first film devoted to this particular subject. In demonstrating that observational learning is both complex and powerful and occurs in both children and adults, includes discussion of Bandura and Walters' famous "Bobo doll" experiment, excerpts from the Papago Indian project to teach concepts by film modeling, and excerpts from a range of modeling therapy films. Shows how such learning, if uncontrolled, can be negative but that, if harnessed, can be useful in both instruction and therapy. 23 min. Color. 1978.

(*One Step at a Time: An Introduction to Behavior Modification*; see Chapter 16.)

Pavlov: The Conditioned Reflex. EMC. Sympathetic portrait of Pavlov and introduction to his work. Includes old photos and films from Russian historical archives. Explains conditioned versus unconditioned reflexes and outlines his contribution to the study of the physiology of higher nervous activity in the brain. 25 min. Color. 1975.

The Power of Positive Reinforcement. CRM. One of CRM's Organizational Behavior series, it documents the systematic on-site application of behavior management at a 3M plant (where $5 million was saved through increased worker efficiency) and an amusement park in Minnesota, the defensive line of the Minnesota Vikings, and the City Sanitation Department in Detroit. 28 min. Color. 1978.

Reward and Punishment. CRM. Presents specific applications of instrumental learning theory to the management of children through a series of photographed examples of children's behavior and narration by James Gardner. Considers the assumptions and rationale behind behavioral techniques used in therapy, education, and child rearing. 14 min. Color. 1974.

Sign On/Sign Off. EMC. Presents basic methods of computer-assisted learning in nontechnical terms. Contrasts standard classroom procedures with sequences at the computer terminal. Presents short descriptions of the tutorial and inquiry methods of computer-assisted learning. Instructive and thorough, though some of the audio is distorted. 24 min. Color. 1967.

To Alter Human Behavior . . . Without Mind Control. EMC. Demonstrates how conditioning techniques have been applied to human behavior, including the conditioning of blood flow in the hand. Discusses controversial aspects of behavior modification such as the use of monetary rewards with young school children and suggests that the potential is present for both promising uses and abuses. 22 min. Color. 1974.

(*Token Economy: Behaviorism Applied*; see Chapter 16.)

Chapter 7 Lecture/Demonstration Suggestions

Chapter 7 is difficult for students. The concepts and terminology are subtle, specific, and new to them. For this chapter you will probably want to stick close to the text, using your time to repeat and clarify what is involved. You can diagram classical and operant conditioning, add examples, answer questions, and whatever else helps, but this is probably not the time to add much new information.

If there are certain basics you want your class to know, you should be sure to note them. One reason for difficulty with this material is that students have a hard time learning all of it and yet are not familiar enough with it to know what the highlights are.

One useful way of contrasting the two major types of conditioning is to go through the terms that are common to them and be sure that students understand the similarities: reinforcement, generalization/discrimination, and so on. Then point out the terms and concepts specific to only one type—for example, shaping. Be sure to point out terms that have different meanings for classical and operant conditioning. In "reinforced" classical trials, for example, the original stimulus is presented, whereas in a "reinforced" operant trial a "reward" is presented. Other aspects of the concept of reinforcement will probably also need elaboration. It is useful, for example, to emphasize that for practical purposes reinforcement is primarily relevant to operant conditioning and essentially equivalent to "reward."

A particular complexity that is often confusing is the relationship between positive reinforcement, negative reinforcement, and punishment. You may wish to elaborate a bit on this. As noted in the text (p. 204), positive reinforcement involves *presenting* a "reward" contingent on behavior that the experimenter wishes to *strengthen*. Negative reinforcement represents essentially the same principle— that is, the strengthening of a desired response by making a reward contingent upon it—but it differs in that the reward is the *termination* of an *aversive* stimulus. According to this definition, escape learning uses "reinforcement" (that is, "reward") in the same way as maze learning with a goal box. "Punishment," on the other hand, means making the onset of an aversive stimulus contingent on behavior that the experimenter desires to *weaken*. Punishment is similar to negative reinforcement only in that both use an aversive stimulus and both arouse undesirable emotional responses, which inhibit learning and add negative affect to the whole learning situation.

For the sake of summarizing, you can use the "on" and "off" of a "plus" or "minus" stimulus. Thus the "on" of a "plus" is positive reinforcement, the "on" of a "minus" is punishment (direct), the "off" of a "minus" is negative reinforcement, and the "off" of a "plus" is also punishment (call it indirect).

You can then note that of the four types, the two using the "plus" are generally preferred, that is, positive reinforcement and what is sometimes called "response cost." As noted, both those using the "minus" have penalties in negative affect, but direct punishment, in addition, has further particular problems. As a way of teaching adaptive behavior it is usually poor, since in addition to the emotional problems, it provides no help in teaching desired responses. Consequently, it may only temporarily suppress undesirable responses without more desirable ones being learned. (For a contemporary review of punishment, see G. C. Walters and J. E. Grusec, *Punishment*, San Francisco: W. H. Freeman and Company, 1977.)

If punishment is appropriately used, however, one can take advantage of these characteristics. If one wants to simply stop ongoing undesired behavior before teaching new behavior, punishment may be very effective. It is in this way that Ivar Lovaas uses it in his behavioral approach to teaching language to autistic children. His well-known use of electric shock devices is to stop disruptive—often self-destructive—acts so that positive reinforcement can be used to shape new and more adaptive responses. (Lovaas' work is included in several films, including *Behavior Modification: Teaching Language to Psychotic Children*, suggested for Chapter 16. For further general reference suitable for students, see *Psychology Today*, January 1974, which includes both a sketch of Lovaas—"Poet with a Cattle Prod"—and a conversation with him—"After You Hit a Child, You Can't Just Get Up and Leave Him; You Are Hooked to That Kid.")

Another component of Chapter 7 is CAL. This topic is notably of interest to students; however, they may have prior opinions—typically negative. The popularized view of behavioral techniques often emphasizes a fear of control and manipulation, so that many entering students are negative toward behavior modification in general and to anything that to them seems similar. They are also concerned with mass, anonymous processing in education. Thus, they may prejudge the notion of CAL as manipulative and designed to force conformity on unwilling students. If you sense this and wish to counteract it, you may want to lecture, show films, or even use a question-and-answer format to do so.

One point to note is the difference between technology and goals; programmed techniques can be used to train independence and creativity, as well as conformity. Another important point concerns the effects on children's self-image. Adults often feel incompetent when confronting complex hardware, including computers, and feel that children must be really intimidated. On the contrary, children may be completely uninhibited with computers. (One user of a computer programmed it to say "Hello" via teletype to his young son when he approached and pressed a key; nonplussed, the boy waved to the typewriter and replied "Hi.") They may even get substantial feelings of personal achievement and competence from being able to control the machine.

CAL is, of course, not limited to younger children. Your students might be interested in its use at the college level—if they are not already using it at your school —as presented in *Change* magazine, March 1976 and in S. G. Smith and B. A. Sherwood, "Educational Uses of the PLATO Computer System," *Science* 192 (23 April 1976): 344–52.

Chapter 7 Short-Essay Questions

1. Define classical conditioning, using a specific procedure as an example and labeling its components appropriately (including at least US, CS, UR, and CR).

2. Define and contrast generalization and discrimination. Are these functions relevant only to classical conditioning?
3. Define operant conditioning, using a specific procedure as an example. In what crucial way(s) does it differ from classical conditioning?
4. Discuss the advantages of partial reinforcement, including the four major reinforcement schedules and their differing effects.
5. Suggest how one might create a conditioned reinforcer (for human beings). Why is this such an important concept?
6. How would you go about shaping a chimp to play a ragtime piano tune? How might related principles be used to help problem children?
7. Explain the differences between positive reinforcement, negative reinforcement, and punishment.
8. What are some of the notable ways that reinforcement via brain-implanted microelectrodes differs from more conventional reinforcement—for example, via food?
9. Give an example of what is meant by insight learning and describe some of the variables known to influence such learning.
10. What are the features of programmed instruction and CAL that make them effective?

CHAPTER 8: REMEMBERING AND FORGETTING

Summary

Chapter 8 begins with the three stages and two types of memory. Short-term memory is then considered, including Critical Discussions on eidetic images and alternative interpretations of retrieval. Long-term memory is discussed, with Critical Discussions of alternative interpretations of imagery findings and biochemical bases of long-term storage. Suggestions are offered for improving memory and the relation between short-term and long-term memory is discussed, including a Critical Discussion on retrograde amnesia. A final section considers constructive aspects of memory.

Chapter 8 Film Suggestions

Human Memory. HBJ. Gordon Bower narrates a graphic demonstration of the processes of memory, memory aids, and the cognitive distortions in reconstructing memory. Considers short- and long-term memory, techniques for memorizing, effective retrieval cues, and the gradual distortions as a story is told and retold. Ends with an admonition to cultivate and treasure memory as the key to our ability to learn. 28 min. Color. 1978.

Information Processing. CRM. A cocktail party hosted by comedian David Steinberg provides the raw material to show how we receive, process, store, and retrieve information. During the frivolity, examples of information overload, limitation of attention, selective attention, refabrication of memory, memory organization, and inappropriate strategies of problem solving are on display. Winner of several awards. 29 min. Color. 1971.

(*Miracle of the Mind*; see Chapter 2.)

(*Three Cognitive Skills: Middle Childhood*; see Chapter 3.)

Chapter 8 Lecture/Demonstration Suggestions

In addition to the references listed at the end of Chapter 8, two more popularized ones offer further material of interest to students that you can incorporate into lectures. Luria's *Mind of a Mnemonist* (New York: Avon Books, 1968) is a fascinating book that you will probably want to add to your professional library. In addition to being the source for the "method of loci," as listed in the text (p. 238), Luria's mnemonist utilized his synesthesia to aid his memory. He also ran into some problems because of his difficulty in *forgetting*; he had to devise a technique to try to deliberately hide or obliterate things he no longer wanted to remember.

In addition, an article in *Psychology Today* (C. F. Stromeyer, III, "Eidetikers," November 1970, pp. 76–80) describes a young instructor at Harvard who is apparently an eidetiker. (See the Critical Discussion on p. 224 of the text.) According to the article, she is capable of reproducing one-half of the computer-generated random-dot patterns that yield three-dimensional shapes so precisely that she can overlap it with a real presentation of the other half and get the 3-D effect.

A demonstration that is useful here, although it can also be used elsewhere in the course, is to give students a quick version of the digit-span test. The limited storage capacity of short-term memory becomes vivid when they can feel the limits, as they can here. The *Study Guide* includes an exercise based on this (p. 128), which you may use as a guide. Or you may simply give them a string of more-or-less-random digits, spoken with even, regular pacing. When you finish, they are to write down the string. Five will be child's play, six easy, seven difficult, in accordance with the concept of the "magic" number 7 ± 2 (discussed in the text on p. 223). The best effect is probably to give them seven digits once or twice, until they can do that easily and then give them nine. Nine is so much harder than seven that as you get to the eighth or ninth digit, the class will tend to gasp or laugh, at the impossibility of it.

If you want to take the time, you can go on to show them how to "chunk" such information (as discussed in the text on p. 226). They may then be able to handle the nine. (You can point out in connection with this that phone numbers are easier to remember because they are already broken into chunks.)

Chapter 8 Short-Essay Questions

1. What are the three stages of memory, that is, the three necessary processes for a sensory input at time A to yield memory at time B?
2. Compare acoustic and visual codes in short-term memory. Which code is dominant and how do we know?
3. Explain what is meant by the magic number seven. How are "chunks" related to this magic number?
4. Compare what the content of an imagery code and a semantic code might be for the word "speedboat."
5. Discuss the two major factors that research has shown to be important in increasing the chances of successful retrieval from long-term memory.
6. Explain the difference between retroactive and proactive interference. How does Freud's concept of repression differ from both of these?
7. Explain the difference between the mnemonic systems called the method of loci and the key-word method. What is it about these techniques that helps memory, that is, what is the common factor?
8. What is retrograde amnesia, and what does it tell us about the organization or functioning of memory?
9. Describe the Atkinson and Shiffrin dual-memory model.
10. Discuss the functioning of inferences, stereotypes, and schemata in the "construction" of memories.

CHAPTER 9: LANGUAGE AND THOUGHT

Summary

Chapter 9 begins with the nature of concepts, including a Critical Discussion on the linguistic relativity hypothesis. It then considers communication, with a Critical Discussion on phrases. Development of language follows, with a Critical Discussion on animal communication. Visual thinking and creativity are also discussed, followed by a final section in problem solving and the simulation of it by computer.

Chapter 9 Film Suggestions

Acquisition of Language by a Speechless Child. EMC. A speechless eight-year-old boy responds accurately to complex language, demonstrating that understanding does not depend on ability to speak. Although he has never used words, he clearly understands complex syntactical structures. His speech defect is "not due to any peripheral motor or anatomic defects," since he vocalizes in an imitative and spontaneous manner. A brief biography explains the child's medical, developmental, and environmental backgrounds. Limited to professional and college course audiences. 17 min. Color. 1962.

(*Behavior Modification: Teaching Language to Psychotic Children*; see Chapter 16.)

Child Language: Learning Without Teaching. EMC. Examines problems children face in mastering the complexity of language. Demonstrations show how children master such markers as tenses and plurals, "before" and "after," the construction of questions, and full sentences. Shows that a child's statements may not mean what an adult thinks they do. With Eve Clark. 15 min. Color.

Communication: The Nonverbal Agenda. CRM. Alerts viewers to the constant interpersonal flow of nonverbal communication and prepares them to recognize the messages they are sending and receiving. Stop-action scenes are used to point out how nonverbal messages can promote misunderstandings, and instruction is given on how to employ nonverbal cues to reinforce spoken words. From the Organizational Behavior collection. 30 min. Color. 1975.

Cybernetics. MH. The similarities of brain and machine are studied by cybernetics, based on analogs between the nervous system and electrical communications systems such as computers. Defines its subject by concrete devices: a mobile machine that simulates human learning, responding to and relating light and sound stimuli; a mechanical mouse learning a maze in one trip; and a dramatic chess game with international grandmaster Laslo Szabo facing a computer. (The computer wins.) Budapest Film Studios. 22 min. Color.

(*Koestler on Creativity*; see Chapter 12.)

Language Development. CRM. How do we so quickly acquire so complex a system of communication? What faculties are we born with? What are the environmental determinants? Includes an animation sequence showing the progression from an infant's crying, cooing, babbling, and echolalic utterances to words. Concludes with Chomsky's theory that the human mind is genetically preprogrammed to process the kinds of information needed to create language. 20 min. Color. 1973.

Language Development. HR. Views the remarkable and orderly process by which a child learns language in the first four years. Begins with initial utterances and examines the development of phonemes, syntax, and semantics. Animation and live action are used to suggest the process by which language is acquired and how that acquisition can be influenced. 24 min. Color.

(*Nonverbal Communication*; see Chapter 11.)

Talk to the Animals. CRM. Shows the progress being made in teaching communication skills to primates in experimental labs at Stanford, Oklahoma University, and the Yerkes Primate Center. Light, fast-moving sequences show the surprising sophistication of primate responses and describe how techniques and tools used in these experiments are being modified for use in teaching handicapped humans. 12 min. Color. 1978.

Talking With Dolphins. EMC. Describes experiments at the U.S. Naval Undersea Research and Development Center in which human speech is electronically changed into underwater "whistle words" to communicate with dolphins. Shows the experimental apparatus, explains how the dolphins were trained, and observes them responding to spoken commands. 16 min. Color. 1970.

Teaching Sign Language to the Chimpanzee Washoe. EMC. Illustrates the teaching of Washoe at the University of Nevada, Reno. Demonstrates the range of Washoe's vocabulary in American Sign Language, including signs for objects, proper names, modifiers, actions, and negatives, the development of sentence-like sequences, and spontaneous comments and questions initiated by Washoe. Consists of research footage interspersed with interviews and commentary by the researchers. Produced by Allen and Beatrice Gardner. 48 min. Black and white. 1973.

(*Three Cognitive Skills: Middle Childhood*; see Chapter 3.)

Chapter 9 Lecture/Demonstration Suggestions

Chapter 9 may be considered to have four major elements with respect to lecture topics: language, visual thinking, problem solving, and simulation of human thinking. While these topics may be covered in a form similar to the text, there are some interesting ways of bringing in other material if you wish to.

One very useful approach to language, for example, is to structure a lecture around Lenneberg's view (*The Biological Foundations of Language*, New York: Wiley, 1967). You need not fully agree with Lenneberg's conclusions to use this. It allows you to contrast innate and learning views of language—for example, Chomsky's and Skinner's—and to offer a synthesis as a resolution. It also allows you to relate language to the content of other chapters—for example, the physiology of Chapter 2, including the specialization of hemispheres, and the developmental sequences of Chapter 3.

An excellent reference for visual thinking is R. H. McKim's *Experiences in Visual Thinking* (Monterey, Calif.: Brooks/Cole, 1972). McKim has summarized his techniques developed as a professor in Stanford's creative engineering design school.

Numerous aspects of problem-solving could be expanded. One is "set" and its effects and ways of breaking sets or being "creative." G. A. Davis and J. A. Scott's book *Training Creative Thinking* (New York: Holt, Rinehart & Winston, 1971) includes several examples of each, as does Adams' book, *Conceptual Blockbusting* (San Francisco: W. H. Freeman, 1974). (A briefer version has appeared with the same title in *The Stanford Magazine*, Spring/Summer 1974, pp. 34–41.) Such "sets" or "blocks" can be used to make other points—for example, implicit sexism, since sets include pre-existing expectations that males will occupy certain roles; the Davis and Scott selections include several problems in which this expectation is the key block to solving the problem.

Also useful is Brewster Ghiselin's collection of first-person reports of successful creative activity—for example, by Einstein and others—from poetry to physics (*The Creative Process*, New York: Mentor, 1952). Many of these reports are interesting in the extent to which language does or does not play a part; Einstein, for example, reports thinking in "muscular" terms. (Such reports are also interesting in terms of their possible relevance to brain hemisphere specialization.)

Simulation of human thinking, of course, leads to robotics. In addition to the films noted on this topic, you may wish to note Turing's test for differentiating human from simulation thought (as described in N. Nievergelt and J. C. Farrar, "What Machines Can and Cannot Do," *American Scientist* 61 (May-June 1973): 309–15). An intriguing article on the capacities achieved by a "robot" of sorts appeared in the November 21, 1971 issue of *Life* ("Meet Shaky, The First Electronic Person"), while useful recent summaries are found in D. Cudhea, "Artificial Intelligence," *The Stanford Magazine*, Spring/Summer 1978, pp. 8+, and B. Raphael, *The Thinking Computer: Mind Inside Matter* (San Francisco: W. H. Freeman, 1976).

Chapter 9 Short-Essay Questions

1. Explain what it means to have a concept, including the aspects of typicality and hierarchy.
2. Describe how a child's overextending the meaning of a word demonstrates the notion of hypothesis testing in language acquisition.
3. Explain the relationships among *predicate, subject, noun phrase, verb phrase,* and *proposition.* Which of these corresponds to a thought?
4. How does a phoneme differ from a morpheme, and how are they combined into a language?
5. Describe the development of a child's speech from gestures to complete sentences. What does the phrase "telegraphic speech" mean in this context?

6. Compare the imitation, conditioning, and hypothesis-testing views of how children learn language.
7. Can other species learn human language? Discuss some of the evidence and show what parts of this evidence would be pointed to by those who believe that other species can or cannot learn language.
8. Describe an experiment by which one could study the operation of mental rotation of images. Does such rotation seem to happen?
9. How can a computer be programmed to simulate human thinking? Explain in terms of the steps used to solve a letter series problem such as RSCDSTDE.
10. Describe the two processes used by the General Problem Solver and how it sequences these.

CHAPTER 10: BASIC DRIVES AND MOTIVES

Summary

Chapter 10 defines motivation and considers instinct, drive-reduction, and incentive approaches, with a Critical Discussion on species-specific behavior. It discusses hunger, with emphasis on hypothalamic regulation, and findings on human obesity, including a Critical Discussion on whether some people are naturally fat. Thirst is discussed, also with consideration of hypothalamic regulation, followed by sex, including homosexuality and transsexualism. Other basic motives of maturation, pain avoidance, and curiosity are considered, followed by the current status of motivational concepts.

Chapter 10 Film Suggestions

Battered Child. EMC. Documentary study shows team of psychiatrists, pediatricians, and social workers studying causes and effects of child abuse. Points out that more children die each year from parental abuse than from all commonly known diseases. Argues that parents who abuse children are often mentally ill themselves and need psychiatric therapy rather than penal action. 58 min. Black and white. 1969.

(*Brain: Creating a Mental Elite*; see Chapter 2.)

Imprinting. EMC. Formation of early social attachments and their biological importance. Black-necked swans and barnacle geese are seen in family social behavior, then with members of another species and with an inanimate object. Laboratory

131

imprinting shows effects of age, rearing conditions, and the characteristics of the imprinting stimulus. 38 min. Color. 1968.

(*Miracle of the Mind*; see Chapter 2.)

The Psychology of Eating. HBJ. Elliot S. Valenstein considers a variety of questions as to why humans eat what, when, and as much as they do, as well as why some become obese and strategies for weight control. Shows that newborns have strong taste preferences and that early experience can affect later preferences. Illustrates conditioned aversion to change eating habits in rats and in controlling wolves' predation of sheep. Demonstrates the roles of external and internal cues, and hypothalamic control, in eating. Ends with discussion of obesity, including exaggerated responsiveness of the obese to external stimuli and behavioral programs to reduce overeating. 29 min. Color. 1978.

Research in Animal Behavior. HR. Shows psychologists, ethologists, and biologists at work, via six classic experiments, including von Frisch's work with the dance language of bees, crowding in Norway rats, and the social behavior of baboons. Not only raises the issue of how much of each species' behavior is biologically programmed, but shows a variety of research methods. 18 min. Color.

Sociobiology: Doing What Comes Naturally. EMC. Surveys research on the biological origins of human behavior. Several biologists and anthropologists explain—citing their research with monkeys, fish, and so on—their theories of male competitiveness and aggression, whether female "sexual reticence" is social or biological, the origins of warfare, and reasons for rebellion of young people. 22 min. Color. 1972.

Some of Your Best Friends. EMC. Sympathetic documentary reveals the discrimination against homosexuals and shows some of the activities of the gay liberation movement. Includes candid interviews with male and female homosexuals, scenes from group meetings, demonstrations, and a gay parade. 38 min. Color. 1972.

Chapter 10 Lecture/Demonstration Suggestions

There are several directions you can take with respect to Chapter 10. You may wish to elaborate on sexual development and behavior, which is of great interest to students. If done carefully, this offers a vehicle not only for considering sexual development from a physiological-motivational perspective, but also for integrating the influence of genetics, environment, and behavior. It is also very useful for considering the differences between the sexes, biological and cultural, known and potential, as background data for questions of sexism.

If you want to do this, a lecture can be developed from John Money's sequence of important sexual development stages and the problems that can occur at each stage. Coverage of this material virtually automatically leads you into the complexity of interaction among genetics, environment, and behavior. The tendency for human issues to involve such interactions is probably one of the major generalizations students should carry away from the introductory course, and this material makes it immediate and relevant. For Money's work, see either his small book *Sex Errors of the Body* (1968) or the larger and more elaborated as well as more up-to-date *Man and Woman, Boy and Girl* (1972), coauthored with Anke Ehrhardt (both Baltimore: Johns Hopkins University Press). (If you do this, you will want to refer back to the genetics material of Chapter 2.) Another book of Money's, coauthored with Patricia Tucker, is *Sexual Signatures: On Being a Man or a Woman* (Boston: Little, Brown and Company, 1975). It is less technical and focuses more on sex roles than *Man and Woman, Boy and Girl.*

For a personal history of the problems faced—and apparently to a large extent overcome—by a well-known transsexual, see Jan Morris' book *Conundrum* (New York: Harcourt Brace Jovanovich, 1974).

You may choose not to get into the sexual development issues, or you may decide to raise these issues in association with another chapter (for example, Chapter 2 or 3). In that case, you may wish to use here the history of one of the major aspects of Chapter 10, the source of hunger cues, as an example of the gradual accumulation of knowledge. *Psychology in the Making* (New York: Knopf, 1962), Postman's collection of histories of concepts in psychology, includes a section by Rosenzweig on hunger. By integrating that material with the recent research covered in the text, you can show how such an area develops—how any answers tend to lead to new questions, how the progress may be irregular and related to other events and/or disciplines, and so on.

Some such sense of history is a useful antidote to a variety of misconceptions, some of them unintentionally fostered by those of us who teach—for example, that progress moves smoothly from one major event to another or that researchers' important findings are always the result of careful planning and hypothesizing. (For a fascinating account of the development of a single important idea, see James D. Watson's *The Double Helix: Being a Personal Account of the Discovery of the Structure of DNA*, New York: Atheneum, 1977.)

Yet another approach might be simply to focus on the hypothalamus. You could refer to the appropriate sections of Chapter 2 for the development and structure, summarize its implications in various motivation areas given in Chapter 10, and refer to possible involvement in the psychological disorders and therapeutic techniques of Chapters 15 and 16.

Chapter 10 Short-Essay Questions

1. What is the relationship said to exist between a need and a drive? How is homeostasis relevant?
2. Compare the three major theories of motivation (instinct, drive-reduction, and incentive). What is the crucial assumption and/or emphasis of each that defines it and sets it apart from the others?
3. What do ethologists study and how? Is there any reason to consider that their work might have implications for humans?
4. What are the functions of the LH and VMH in controlling food intake? How are the functions of these areas studied experimentally?
5. What variables influence short-term and long-term hypothalamic control of food intake? (Stomach fullness, for example, is one such variable.) What information from the body is used for each? (Stomach distortion and stomach contractions, for example, jointly provide the information for the sensing of stomach fullness.)
6. What differences have been found between the responses of obese and normal individuals to internal and external hunger cues?
7. Discuss the related functions of osmoreceptors and volumetric receptors in the hypothalamus.
8. What general function do the sex hormones serve with regard to sexual behavior? (Do they directly elicit specific behaviors, for example?) How does their influence differ from lower to higher species and from males to females of these various species?
9. What has been found with regard to the tendency of animals to explore and manipulate their environment? What are the implications of these findings for drive-reduction theory?
10. What can be said as a summation of the current status of motivational concepts? (Include discussion of the concept of arousal level.)

CHAPTER 11: HUMAN MOTIVATION AND EMOTION

Summary

Chapter 11 begins with a contrast between two different approaches to human motivation: psychoanalytic theory versus social learning theory. It uses these approaches to consider the problem of aggression, including a Critical Discussion on humans as aggressive animals. Specific discussion of issues and theories of emotion are considered next, with a Critical Discussion on lie detection, followed by emotional expression and how emotions can be adaptive or disruptive.

Chapter 11 Film Suggestions

Animal War and Animal Peace. EMC. Examines aggressive behavior, particularly territorial, and self-restraint in conflict among various animal species, including antelopes, herring gulls, and stickleback fish. Discusses differences between animal and human aggressiveness, and shows several methods used to investigate animal behavior. 30 min. Color. 1969.

Children's Aggression: Its Origin and Control. EMC. Studies the types and causes of normal aggression in young children and presents methods of promoting and fostering socially positive behavior through reinforcement and modeling. Distinguishes self-assertion from instrumental, emotional, or hostile aggression, and defines such causes of aggressive behavior as instinct, frustration, and conceptions of self-esteem. 15 min. Color.

Constructive Use of the Emotions. EMC. From the Management Development Series. Sherman Kingsbury, consultant with Arthur D. Little, Inc., surveys the emotions that are accompanied by involuntary physiological reactions. He discusses anxiety and typical responses to it. Fighting and loving are "active" responses, he maintains, because they are attempts to move toward relationships. Withdrawal, however, is a "passive" response and he concludes that "if learning is the game, then passivity is the enemy." 22 min. Color. 1970.

Emotional Development: Aggression. CRM. An evocative probe into the root causes of aggression. A psychologist analyzes an unrehearsed act of aggression in a nursery school—and the reaction of the teacher who inadvertently rewards the aggressor. The film's premise is that the potential for human beings to behave aggressively may be innate, but that the nature, form, timing, and extent of aggression depend greatly on learning. Also explores the relationship between individual aggression and the collective aggression that we call war. 20 min. Color. 1973.

Human Aggression. HR. Vividly depicts the spontaneous aggression of real-life incidents and relates them to scientific principles and laboratory findings. Includes activities of a youth gang, Bard on psychological training of police, Bandura and Walters' work with group influences, and Syke and Matza on the legitimization of aggression in delinquent groups. One of a series by Stanley Milgram. 22 min. Color.

Nonverbal Communication. HR. Examines the scientific findings on communication through gesture, body posture, intonation, eye contact, and facial expression. Includes interviews with Hall on interpersonal distance, Argyle on the equilibrium theory of eye contact, Rosenthal on sex differences in the perception of nonverbal behavior, Akaret on expressions in photographs, and Eibl-Eibesfeldt on biological programming. One of a series by Stanley Milgram. 22 min. Color.

135

(*Observational Learning*; see Chapter 7.)

(*Personality: Early Childhood*; see Chapter 3.)

Chapter 11 Lecture/Demonstration Suggestions

Two major possible lecture topics from Chapter 11 are aggression and emotional labeling. The contrast between psychoanalytic and social-learning views of the sources and handling of aggression is important for students to understand. Arguments about aggression often seem to invoke these views without either being noted specifically; the popularization of Freudian concepts has made them a part of folklore, while imitation of modeled behavior is a common concept. The CRM film *Emotional Development: Aggression* nicely presents this contrast, as well as noting the ethological perspective and offering a synthesis of innate tendencies and learned outlets.

In this connection, you may wish to point out how we all have implicit personality theories, including developmental and motivational theories, that have been presented to us by our culture and that we have absorbed, often without realizing it. For students of this generation, much of this implicit material is quasi-psychoanalytic; not only will they not recognize it as such, but they may not recognize it as theory. That aggression has to be somehow "released," for example, is sure to figure in any discussion of such topics as violence on TV. If the social-learning view is presented, students may try to integrate the two, not recognizing that they are in conflict at a theoretical level.

In noting the existence of implicit theories, you can also point out their subtlety; that which is taken as a "given" may never be questioned. This point is made in Chapter 18 in connection with implicit racism and sexism. Mention of it now can prepare the way for that chapter—at which time you can refer to this one. (You might also use a recent news clipping to demonstrate implicit theories or might ask them to look for one.)

In connection with emotion, one very easy demonstration that can get a lecture off to a roaring start is to arouse their emotions without warning and then ask them to introspect on the changes. If you can change the emotion very quickly, so much the better; you will then be able to use this to discuss one of Cannon's objections to the James-Lange theory.

Since this chapter is a bit more than halfway through the text, you may have recently completed a midterm exam. Even if you have not, exam and grading anxiety is typically not very difficult to arouse. Thus, one way of obtaining, then switching, an emotional reaction is to begin the class with an "announcement" that the grade curve you have planned is entirely too lenient, that someone has to put meaning back into an A grade, and that therefore you are going to . . . and give them some grade expectation as negative as you can manage, without it being transparently preposterous.

As they begin to react, with muttering, shuffling, or outright lynch threats, tell them gently that they've been put on—that what you threatened is not true, but that today's topic is emotions, and . . . . They will quickly recognize the situation, and the tenor will change to relief, mixed with residual hostility for having been tricked. Go with it. Ask them to offer specific labels for what emotion they felt initially and list them on the board. If they are hesitant about expressing anger, suggest that it is a reasonable label; they will agree. You will probably be able to spot and note ambiguity—difficulty in deciding what was felt, as well as difficulty in picking the appropriate label for it. Then ask them what happened when you noted that it was a trick; ask for another set of labels and note that their arousal continued, though the label changed.

You are then set up with much of what you need as an introduction to James-Lange, Cannon-Bard, and Singer-Schachter. The entire process takes only a few minutes, is instructive, and wakes up your students. If you are sure to point out that you would, in fact, not make arbitrary and capricious changes in grading but recognize this as an emotional area for them, you should be able not only to defuse any residual hostility but to achieve greater rapport. After all, the relief from threat is also a powerful reinforcer.

Chapter 11 Short-Essay Questions

1. Describe Maslow's proposals for classifying human motives.
2. Describe Freud's psychoanalytic theory of motivation.
3. Describe the social-learning theory of motivation.
4. What are the implications of assuming aggression to be a drive? What evidence is there for such a position?
5. How do social-learning theorists view aggression? (Do they consider it a drive?)
6. Describe how the psychoanalytic theory of motivation differs from the social-learning theory, using their differing views of aggression and catharsis as an example. How do these differences lead to different implications for society in dealing with aggression?
7. What was the James-Lange theory of emotion, and how does it differ from the Cannon-Bard theory?
8. What is Schachter's cognitive-physiological theory of emotion, and what is the research evidence for it?
9. Is emotional expression innate or culturally determined? What research evidence can you cite to support your answer?
10. What are some of the variables that determine whether emotional arousal will be beneficial or detrimental in performing some task?

CHAPTER 12: MENTAL ABILITIES AND THEIR MEASUREMENT

Summary

Chapter 12 first considers testing itself, contrasting aptitude and achievement tests and noting the need for reliability and validity. It focuses on the specific issue of intelligence testing: definitions, tests, relationship to creativity, age changes, genetic basis, extremes reached, and the present status of ability testing. Critical Discussions consider culture-fair tests and issues of racial differences and intelligence.

Chapter 12 Film Suggestions

Intelligence: A Complex Concept. CRM. Demonstrates the many popular concepts of intelligence with filmed questions of people on the street; their answers reveal the widespread confusion between what intelligence is as tests measure it and what intelligence is in everyday life. Then explores some of the varied definitions, including Piaget's and Guilford's, discusses the problems inherent in testing and shows a variety of test types. 20 min. Color. 1978.

IQ Myth. EMC. Examines ways in which the IQ concept has been used and abused, focusing on the question of how much importance, if any, should be placed on the result of a single test. Studies the tests themselves and uses interviews with psychologists, teachers, and others to show the cultural, racial, and social class biases of the tests. Criticizes Arthur Jensen's theories. CBS News production. 51 min. Color. 1975.

Janet Is a Little Girl. EMC. Severely retarded (Down's syndrome) children in an innovative, highly successful program to develop language skills and teach reading. Begun in 1959, with ten hospitalized children under five months old, later compared to a group reared by parents. Comparisons at two and five years old showed the hospitalized children falling behind; then the five-year enrichment program began. Three years later, nine of the ten previously nonverbal hospitalized children were speaking in sentences and reading an average of 200 words; average IQs of the two groups were essentially identical. Classroom scenes show how the hospitalized children were taught to speak, read, and play music games. The patience, understanding, and affection of the staff are clearly evident. 28 min. Black and white. 1972.

Koestler on Creativity. EMC. Noted writer Arthur Koestler discusses his theories concerning the conscious and unconscious processes underlying creativity, emphasizing scientific discovery but considering artistic originality as well. Visually imaginative sequences intercut with the discussion clarify, give examples, and lend force to the ideas presented. 40 min. Black and white. 1971.

They Call Me Names. EMC. Demonstrates that young people stereotyped as "mentally retarded" are often perfectly capable of understanding that they are considered inferior—and therefore become dispirited and act accordingly. Specialists and parents tell of the pain and discouragement such young people feel, and also describe recent efforts to provide a more normal living environment for them than traditional custodial care. 20 min. Color. 1972.

Understanding the Gifted. EMC. Observes gifted children from the fourth through the twelfth grades, showing techniques of interview and group discussion. Examines their ability to handle symbols and generalizations, their creativeness, the frequent multiplicity of interests, and the high ideals and values so often found among them, but also considers some negative traits. 33 min. Color. 1965.

Chapter 12 Lecture/Demonstration Suggestions

Intelligence testing is becoming a very sensitive issue for today's students. Many of them are already extensively "politicized" on the topic, with little or no knowledge of the facts. The material in Chapter 12 includes a lot of good, solid factual grounding but you may still encounter emotional resistance or questioning.

The best approach is probably to note that, in general, the use made of any technological advance can be good or bad. The social desirability of the use of knowledge is, at least to a large extent, separable from the knowledge itself. You can point out that testing, including IQ testing, can be intrusive, that it can be poorly done, and that it can be used in inappropriate ways. You can also point out that it can be a very useful tool. Your students will probably not have realized, for example, that the only way one can recognize problems, treat them, and measure the results with any precision is to have criterion measures. Point out that numerous genetic and environmental threats—for example, oxygen deficiency, lead poisoning—can lead to mental retardation and that diagnosis, aid, and prevention of such retardation utilizes IQ testing. (In discussing the uses of IQ testing you might find valuable the opinions of William Raspberry, a columnist for the Washington *Post*. In a *Newsweek* editorial ("Testing Minorities," 23 September 1974, p. 19) Raspberry, who is black, advocates not elimination of tests but improvement in their use.)

The use made of the end product—that is, IQ scores—however, is only the final step. It is helpful to diagram for your students, on the board or in a passout, the other steps involved in order to show where assumptions and sources of error enter. This sequence can be expressed as:

$$\text{PARENTS} \xrightarrow{1} \text{GENETIC IQ} \xrightarrow{2} \text{LIFE EXPERIENCES} \xrightarrow{3} \text{INNER IQ} \xrightarrow{4}$$
$$\text{IQ TEST} \xrightarrow{5} \text{IQ SCORE}$$

The final score is what you have to work with, for a given person, but much precedes it. At arrow 1 there is a selection of genetic material at conception; you can mention problems of faulty genes, environmentally induced chromosome damage, and so on. "Genetic IQ" tends then to be the maximum potential, given a reasonable environment; most environmental influences that we know of tend to be negative and reduce IQ. But in a few cases doctors can improve on the genetics—for example, by preventing retardation from PKU. It is probable that in the future more such improvement will be possible, but for now the "Genetic IQ" tends to be the maximum one on the diagram, with most points of "slippage" thereafter yielding lower results. (You might at this point refer back to the genetics material of Chapter 2.)

"Life Experiences" includes both prenatal and postnatal experiences, with some of the former being crucial—for example, the mother's diet. If all these experiences are ideal, the child will develop to genetic maximum, but obviously in very few cases will every element be perfect. (It is conceivable that we are nearly all slightly brain-damaged from oxygen deficiency at birth, for example; until we figure out how to prevent it, how would you know that your genetics did not provide a much higher IQ than what you now score?)

"Inner IQ" represents the net real capability of a particular individual at a particular time, say just at the instant that an IQ test is to be given. Note that many sources of variation have entered in so far and we still have not reached the test stage. (Incidentally, the term IQ is a misnomer, used here only as a shorthand for "intelligence"; you can use other terminology if you wish.) "Inner IQ" is made up of whatever complex of processing capabilities, memories, and so on, that one wishes to define.

That definition is the first step necessary in creating an IQ test; it is at least implicit in any such test. Arrow 4 marks test design; "slippage" here includes the problems of definition, as well as the operationalizing of them and validation of the result. Any particular test that results is only one of many possible ways of measuring the "Inner IQ" of an individual.

Arrow 5 then, of course, represents all the problems of test administration, the point at which subject motivation, tester competence, tester-subject interactions, and other factors enter. This is the point that is typically criticized by those who are too sophisticated to simply condemn tests outright, but it obviously is only the final step in the sequence yielding an IQ score.

You might also note in summary that the steps through arrow 3 actually influence the person's intellectual capability, while arrows 4 and 5 represent the measuring of this capacity; these are two quite different issues.

Chapter 12 Short-Essay Questions

1. How do aptitude tests differ from achievement tests? In what way are they inevitably related?
2. What is meant by the reliability and the validity of a test, and why must a test have *both* to be acceptable?
3. What terms are entered into the "quotient" of the "intelligence quotient," and what are the assumptions that led to measuring intelligence in this way?
4. What is meant by culture-fair intelligence tests, and what are some of the problems with work done on them to date?
5. Describe and contrast Spearman's proposal of *g* and *s* factors and Thurstone's proposed set of primary abilities as explanations of intelligence. What can you say about which is "right," according to available evidence?
6. Describe the changes in IQ likely to take place in a person's lifetime. Include factors that could cause this to differ for different people.
7. How can you assess the importance of genetic factors in intelligence? What is the general relation found by such assessment?
8. What are some of the important issues involved in assessing whether there are racial differences in intelligence? What general conclusions can be drawn despite these issues?
9. What different causes have been proposed for relatively mild and general retardation versus the more severe forms of retardation? (Hint: What specific terms have been used to label these different types so as to suggest these different causes?)
10. Describe some of the results of the Terman long-term study of gifted children. How do these contradict stereotypes of the very bright child?

CHAPTER 13: PERSONALITY AND ITS ASSESSMENT

Summary

Chapter 13 begins with a discussion of the forces shaping personality: both common and unique experiences. It analyzes and compares four theoretical perspectives: trait, social learning, psychoanalytic, and phenomenological approaches. Personality assessment techniques are considered, with Critical Discussions of controls for faking and the "Barnum effect." Issues in the consistency of personality follow, with some final suggestions for an integrated view of personality.

Chapter 13 Film Suggestions

(*A Conversation with B. F. Skinner*; see Chapter 7.)

Dependence: A New Definition. CRM. Explains the psychoanalytic theory of the manner in which we develop healthy dependencies and what happens if we do not. It also proposes that freedom comes from the ability to form healthy dependencies, and that unrest during adolescence can be attributed to the search for one's own dependencies. 20 min. Color. 1972.

(*Dialogues: Dr. Carl Rogers* (Parts I and II); see Chapters 16 and 18.)

Individual Differences. CRM. Explores the broad range of human characteristics that are considered normal. Shows tests devised to separate personality differences from traits that indicate developmental problems, including the Denver Developmental Screening Test and the Gesell Infant Test. 16 min. Color. 1978.

Maslow and Self-Actualization (Parts I and II). PCR. Dimensions of self-actualization; recent research and theory.
Part I: *Honesty, Awareness.* Honesty expressed in a sense of humor, social interest, and love. Awareness expressed in efficient perception, freshness of appreciation, the peak experience, and ethical awareness. 30 min. Color. 1969.
Part II: *Freedom, Trust.* Freedom expressed in detachment, creativeness, and spontaneity. Trust expressed in a life mission, autonomy of culture and environment, and acceptance of human nature. 30 min. Color. 1969.

(*Moral Development*; see Chapter 17.)

My Childhood. PCR. Gives insight into the disparity in the American community by showing two boys: Hubert Humphrey (white, middle class, and living in a small town) and James Baldwin (Negro, lower class, and living in an urban slum). Narration provided by Humphrey and Baldwin as they recall their boyhoods. 51 min. Black and white. 1967.

(*Observational Learning*; see Chapter 7.)

Personality. CRM. An unusually articulate and self-aware college senior is the subject of this film. Begins with a self-report contrasted with opinions of his parents, his girl friend, and his roommate. Then explains a person's multiple roles and demonstrates their interaction. Next, personality evaluation by psychologists is noted and techniques such as the "Draw a Person" test and the Thematic Apperception Test are shown. 30 min. Color. 1971.

(*Personality: Adolescence*; see Chapter 3.)

(*Personality: Early Childhood*; see Chapter 3.)

(Personality: Middle Childhood; see Chapter 3.)

Sigmund Freud: His Offices and Home, Vienna. EMC. Depicts Freud's office and home, using a celebrated series of photographs taken before he left Vienna in 1938 to escape the Nazis. Includes an interview with the photographer who took the original pictures, plus old clips of the Nazi occupation of Vienna and the resulting wave of anti-Semitic terrorism. Award winner. 17 min. Color. 1975.

(Three Approaches to Psychotherapy; see Chapter 16.)

Chapter 13 Lecture/Demonstration Suggestions

One obvious demonstration for Chapter 13 is to show the "Barnum effect" (see text p. 404), using Ulrich's phony personality-test results (R. E. Ulrich, T. J. Stachnik, and N. R. Stainton. "Student Acceptance of Generalized Personality Interpretations," *Psychological Reports* 13 (1963): 831–34).

> You have a strong need for other people to like you and for them to admire you. You have a tendency to be critical of yourself. You have a great deal of unused energy which you have not turned to your advantage. While you have some personality weaknesses, you are generally able to compensate for them. Your sexual adjustment has presented some problems for you. Disciplined and controlled on the outside, you tend to be worrisome and insecure inside. At times you have serious doubts as to whether you have made the right decision or done the right thing. You prefer a certain amount of change and variety and become dissatisfied when hemmed-in by restrictions and limitations. You pride yourself as being an independent thinker and do not accept other opinions without satisfactory proof. You have found it unwise to be too frank in revealing yourself to others. At times you are extroverted, affable, sociable, while at other times you are introverted, wary, and reserved. Some of your aspirations tend to be pretty unrealistic.

RATINGS OF PERSONALITY INTERPRETATIONS

Total	Excellent	Good	Average	Poor	Very Poor
Psychologist's Interpretations					
57	27	26	3	1	0
Student's Interpretations					
79	29	30	15	5	0

There are several ways of using this material. You can simply report the study, of course, but that has limited dramatic appeal; or you can suggest to the class that they imagine that they have been given a personality test, and you are now going to read the results, asking them to judge whether the results fit them. They, of course, know that this is an "as if" situation and while this is better than the first option, it is not as powerful as if they had been given a phony test.

Since the manipulations Ulrich went through to convince subjects would be a lot of work for a simple demonstration, you probably don't want to try that, though if by chance they have been given any recent test that could be so construed you might capitalize on it. What you can do, however, is to ask for a single volunteer and "test" the volunteer; ask for a couple of sentence completions, perhaps a handwriting sample, even a phony Rorschach or TAT if you want to be fancy. Be careful to avoid embarrassing your subject, of course. You might ask that the answers be written; this would simultaneously protect the subject from analysis by the class and leave the rest in the dark as to the kind of information you obtained. Suitable "ums" and "a-ha's" while studying the results might help build an atmosphere, providing your acting skills are adequate to bring it off with a straight face.

Then "analyze" the volunteer. While it is best to have memorized it, you can refer to the personality description for help by slipping it over your notes. With suitable pauses for reflection, the exact version used by Ulrich and others can be made to sound off-the-cuff. If your acting skills are, in fact, adequate to the task, the class should be convinced—at least for a while. As you continue to draw conclusions and as they begin to recognize the generality of your conclusions, the sharper ones will realize what you have done, and by the end the whole class probably will have.

You can then, of course, talk not only about the "Barnum effect" but about problems intrinsic to personality testing—for example, the "base rate" and the tendency of people to be "satisfied customers." Point out that the statements in the "test results" came from newsstand astrology books and that most students in the original study found the statements not only valid but helpful. (See the data from the study as summarized above.) People show the same effect, of course, in response to a variety of manipulations. See also the discussion of *The Skeptical Inquirer* articles in the lecture/demonstration suggestions for Chapter 6; Bainbridge's article is relevant here also (W. S. Bainbridge, "Biorhythms: Evaluating a Pseudoscience," *The Skeptical Inquirer*, Spring/Summer 1978, pp. 40–56), as is one by R. W. Bastedo, "An Empirical Test of Popular Astrology," *The Skeptical Inquirer*, Fall 1978, pp. 17–38.

In relating personality testing to theories, you may also wish to point out, if you did not do so in connection with Chapter 11, our tendency to have implicit personality theories, residue from popularized psychological theories.

Chapter 13 Short-Essay Questions

1. Compare the effects of common and unique experiences in shaping a personality.
2. Describe how factor analysis has been used to study personality and why this approach is consistent with trait theory.
3. Discuss the factors that social learning theorists believe are important contributors to a person's behavior, including the different kinds of reinforcement that may be applicable.
4. Describe the three major systems that Freud said made up personality, and explain how they were said to interact.
5. What criticisms of Freud's original theories have been made by later psychoanalysts and others?
6. Discuss the role of the self as phenomenological personality theorists see it.
7. What, in summary, are the most important differences among the basic personality theories of social learning, psychoanalytic, and phenomenological theorists?
8. Compare the general features of the three categories of personality assessment: observational methods, personality inventories, and projective techniques.
9. What are some of the criticisms of projective tests, and how successful have advocates been in answering these?
10. Explain the consistency issue in personality and describe some of the current approaches to this problem.

CHAPTER 14: CONFLICT AND STRESS

Summary

Chapter 14 defines conflict situations and the frustration and reactions to frustration that result. It notes and describes the consequent anxiety, the ways that anxiety can be manifested, and methods for coping with it. Special consideration is given to defense mechanisms, including ways that they can be adaptive as well as maladaptive. It concludes with a discussion of the effects of stress, including Critical Discussions of biofeedback and ways to measure life stress.

Chapter 14 Film Suggestions

(*Battered Child*; see Chapter 10.)

Biofeedback: Listening to Your Head. EMC. Explores the nature, effects, and uses of biofeedback. Explains alpha and theta waves. Interviews a neurophysiologist and a composer and visits a yoga-biomeditation service inside an inflated plastic temple in the Los Angeles hills. 22 min. Color. 1973.

(*Constructive Use of the Emotions*; see Chapter 11.)

(*Depression: A Study in Abnormal Behavior*; see Chapter 15.)

Depression/Suicide: "You Can Turn Bad Feelings Into Good Ones!" EMC. Studies the leading cause of death among teenagers, as young people who have contemplated or attempted suicide discuss their experiences, the causes of their depression, and the methods they have used to prevent such feelings of loneliness or sadness from again overwhelming them. 24 min. Color. 1976.

Learn to Live With Stress: Programming the Body for Health. EMC. Introduction to the psychological and physiological effects of stress on the human organism, with a focus on arteriosclerosis. Includes commentary by Hans Selye and Herbert Benson, interviews with air traffic controllers, who are subject to constant acute stress, and dissections that demonstrate the impact of stress on rats. 22 min. Color. 1974.

(*Neurotic Behavior: A Psychodynamic View*; see Chapter 15.)

Chapter 14 Lecture/Demonstration Suggestions

Chapters 14 through 16 contain some of the most interesting and personally relevant information for students. For some of them, questions of their own and/or others' normalcy are the specific reason for taking the course. This means that you have built-in interest, but it can also cause you certain problems.

One problem is the so-called medical-student syndrome, the tendency to believe that you are experiencing the disease you are reading about. Here it is especially subtle, for, as Chapter 14 points out, we all *do* tend to utilize defense mechanisms. A brief mention to your students of the general tendency toward this syndrome, and a suggestion not to let it worry them, is very strongly recommended at this point in the course. You may even want to mention it once here, in connection with Chapter 14, then repeat it as you move on to the more serious problems of Chapter 15.

A related problem concerns those students who *do* have serious problems. Those who have taught abnormal psychology are familiar with the tendency of students with problems to seek information from that course. But often it cannot be taken without having previously taken introductory psychology, which means that they will be in your course as well, and especially interested in this material.

There are several reasons for noting this problem. For one, you may wish to be careful of any implication of "all of us normals are going to study the crazies," since this will put substantial pressure on those few who tend to consider *themselves* the "crazies." For another, you may get after-class or office visits from these students, asking for help. This request for help may be overt or hidden; if you are alert to the possibilities, you are obviously in a better position to recognize and be able to deal with disturbed students. Finally, you may wish to consider approaching this latter problem directly. In conjunction with the medical-student syndrome warning, you can add that some people do have problems; what you suggest will depend on your own specialization, your school's counseling system, the availability of low-cost community mental health facilities, and so on. You might suggest that students "shop" for a therapist until they find one they get along with.

Note that all of these comments apply to Chapters 14 through 16. It is up to you to decide how much to say when as you cover this material. The last comment, for example, concerning shopping for therapists, could be integrated into the discussion of the different therapy types given in Chapter 16.

The content of Chapter 14 likely to need elaboration is the discussion of defense mechanisms. At the theoretical level, you might wish to contrast the view—essentially derived from the psychoanalytic approach—that defense mechanisms can be used in adaptive ways, with the view—which a social learning theorist might provide—that normal coping strategies can be overused. The net result is similar, except that the flavor of the first is the "pathology of the average," whereas that of the second is "pathology as the extremes of normal." (Note, in connection with this, the Critical Discussion in Chapter 16 (p. 500) contrasting the "mental illness" and "maladaptive habits" views of abnormal psychology.)

Another important point concerning defense mechanisms is the difficulty one may have in labeling a particular case as one mechanism rather than another. The example of reaction formation given in Figure 14-4 (p. 429), for example—the antivivisectionist letter—might also be said to represent projection.

If you wish, you can continue from that point to a more generalized warning about the problem of labels and/or hypothetical constructs becoming explanations. You may have already done so earlier in the course, perhaps in conjunction with a discussion of the scientific method as suggested for Chapter 1. But it is in connection with deviant behavior that this problem may be frequently and strongly seen. One sequence of steps may be noted on the board to illustrate this problem:

OBSERVATION → DESCRIPTION → HYPOTHETICAL CONSTRUCT →
"AS IF" → BELIEF IN CONSTRUCT → CONSTRUCT AS EXPLANATION

(To complete the loop, draw an arrow from explanation back around to the original observation.) By working through this sequence using "crazy" and then perhaps some more professional terms (pick one, as most potentially suffer from this problem) you can show the dangers of labeling. (You can also add an example from another area and note that this sequence was what led to the scientific disrepute of the term "instinct" and its replacement with "species-specific behavior" and that similar criticism has been made of trait labels such as "honesty.")

Finally, in considering the defense mechanisms themselves, you may wish to categorize them. Some, for example, can be considered to be relatively "naive" (for example, denial, repression, or reaction formation), whereas others are more "sophisticated" (for example, rationalization or intellectualization). (You might point out that the latter are likely to be the ones that both you and your students will tend to resort to.)

Chapter 14 Short-Essay Questions

1. What is meant by an approach-avoidance conflict? In what areas of American life are you most likely to encounter such conflicts?
2. What are some of the immediate reactions to frustrations (for example, as shown by the children restricted to the half-toys)?
3. Describe when and how people show an apathy reaction and explain how this may be related to the study of learned helplessness in animals.
4. Compare Freud's theory of anxiety and that of the social learning theorists.
5. What is meant by coping strategies and defensive strategies? Explain both their similarities and their differences.
6. Describe what is meant by a defense mechanism. What precautions would you want to follow in using this concept?
7. In what way are the defense mechanisms of denial and repression similar and in what way are they different?
8. In what way are the defense mechanisms of projection and reaction formation similar and in what way are they different?
9. Are defense mechanisms always maladaptive? Discuss, with examples if possible.
10. Discuss some of the variables with respect to stressful situations that seem to cause or to minimize the development of psychosomatic problems, such as ulcers.

CHAPTER 15: ABNORMAL PSYCHOLOGY

Summary

Chapter 15 notes the variety of definitions of abnormal behavior (statistical, social, and so on) and the major symptomatic categories: neuroses, psychoses, and personality disorders. It considers each of these three categories in detail, giving definitions, descriptions, examples, and so on, and noting the probable incidence and the magnitude of the social cost of these problems. Separate sections consider research on the causes of schizophrenia and problems of alcoholism and drug abuse, while Critical Discussions cover mental disorders and the law plus the current status of diagnostic categories, with reference to DSM-III.

Chapter 15 Film Suggestions

(*Battered Child*; see Chapter 10.)

Depression: A Study in Abnormal Behavior. CRM. Follows a young housewife-teacher through a depressive illness: her inability to function normally; her husband's attempt to ignore her erratic behavior; her severely depressed state; her suicidal threat; his decision to get help; the process of diagnosis, hospitalization, and treatment; her eventual release back into society with symptoms gone; her need for continuing follow-up therapy. Shows the three major short-term therapies—drugs, shock, and group therapy—while stressing that the current trend in treatment is to blend different approaches and therapies. 26 min. Color. 1973.

The Maze. EMC. Part of a set of acclaimed films by James B. Maas designed to demonstrate phenomena and stimulate thinking. An insightful documentary on the life and mental agony of Canadian painter William Kurelik, who struggled in his art to overcome the mental illness from which he suffered. Shows many examples of his work and traces the story of his recovery. Sympathetic and fascinating portrait. Award winner. 30 min. Color. 1971.

Neurotic Behavior: A Psychodynamic View. CRM. Takes a brief episode in the life of a 19-year-old college sophomore, Peter, and shows how his "neurotic" behavior is linked to anxiety from without and childhood memories from within. Through alternating animation and flashbacks, the film portrays, describes, and analyzes the successive stages and defense mechanisms: anxiety, then repression, rationalization, displacement, and, finally, the phobic fears and the obsessive-compulsive neurosis that result. 19 min. Color. 1973.

Schizophrenia: A Shattered Mirror. EMC. Discusses the possible causes of schizophrenia; the tests to communicate with the schizophrenic; drug, shock, and psychological treatment; biochemical and neurophysiological aspects of the disease; and the question of whether the distorted perceptions of a schizophrenic are the result or cause of the disease. A patient now well enough to live outside an institution describes the feelings and effects of schizophrenia. (An older film, to some extent out of date.) 60 min. Black and white. 1966.

The Thin Edge Series. EMC. A five-part series exploring the characteristics of mental health and illness by studying five psychological traits that are part of every normal person's makeup. Each program isolates a particular trait, showing how it can become a mental problem and what treatments are available. Each film is 59 min. Color. 1975.
Aggression: The Explosive Emotion.
Anxiety: The Endless Crisis.
Depression: The Shadowed Valley.
Guilt: The Psychic Censor.
Sexuality: The Human Heritage.

Chapter 15 Lecture/Demonstration Suggestions

The material of Chapter 15 tends to be complex and subtle in its distinctions; it is relatively new to students and of substantial interest. Your best overall plan is probably to stick with this material, emphasizing and repeating as necessary. Consider the suggestions given below as supplementary details or accents.

The lecture suggestions for Chapter 14 are, of course, also applicable here, and, in fact, are even more necessary in this direct discussion of abnormal psychology. The medical-student syndrome and potential problems with disturbed students are more crucial, and an understanding of the problems of labeling is even more necessary.

An aspect of the labeling problem not mentioned before is specifically applicable here. When persons are labeled as being seriously disturbed, whatever the subcategory used, the behavior of others toward them changes and their own self-image may be affected. One important result is that attribution tendencies "flip-flop." So long as one is presumed normal, any bizarre action is viewed as the exception and onlookers tend to attribute it to acceptable causes—for example, fatigue, drugs, initiation rites, and so on. But once abnormality is labeled and thus expected, even perfectly conventional behavior tends to be reinterpreted as evidence of the abnormality. Before a person is labeled, a substantial amount of deviant behavior may be overlooked; after labeling, normal behavior is often ignored or reinterpreted. The magnitude of this problem was one of the powerful aspects of David Rosenhan's *Science* article "On Being Sane in Insane Places," *Science* 179 (1973): 250–58, and one of the reasons for its fame. (See also the Critical Discussion in Chapter 17, p. 543, of the text.)

In addition to the problems of labeling, it might be useful to note some of the intrinsic difficulties of using case histories as data. Case histories are always fascinating, but they do not tell us to what extent they are representative—and may be most interesting to the extent that they are *not* representative. They also suffer from several sources of built-in bias: the acceptance of a case by a therapist, the particular aspects of the case that are noted, the interpretation of these aspects, and the choice of facts to be included in a published summary. Yet, even then, one can often find evidence in a case for another perspective than the one for which the case is presented. There is no doubt of the value of case histories, but those unfamiliar with them need to know what they do and do not represent.

A problem that underlies the public view of disturbed persons is that of their dangerousness to others. It is one of the major reasons for fearing and avoiding them and is often a reason, explicit or implicit, for their commitment. You may wish to elaborate on this point, since it is not specifically considered in this way in Chapter 15 (although it is relevant, for example, to the Critical Discussion on "Mental Disorders and the Law," p. 474). Two aspects of this problem are especially worth noting: (a) The most dangerous individuals are probably those who are at the same time the least "crazy" in a conventional sense, the psychopaths; and (b) despite the occasional paranoid schizophrenic who kills someone as an apparent result of this "illness," diagnosed mental patients as a whole have a lower rate of violence than the community from which they come. (For a general coverage of such issues, see D. T. Lunde's *Murder and Madness*, San Francisco: San Francisco Book Co., 1976.)

Both Chapters 15 and 16 are appropriate for a discussion of the complexity of interaction of causes. In terms of abnormal behavior, for example, the interaction includes genetics and the resulting biochemical activity, as well as environmental factors, both historical and current, including the labeling problem. For Chapter 16 it is most appropriate in terms of the interaction of treatment variables (specifically discussed on p. 507 of that chapter).

A specific technique for relating the text material to the daily world, applicable to both Chapters 15 and 16, is the use of appropriate newspaper clippings. If you keep a clipping file, you can use some of the more outstanding ones to illustrate points. By checking any major metropolitan paper for a few days, you can usually obtain useful current examples. If your students have ready access to such a paper, you can ask them to look for examples—as an assignment, for discussion in class, or however you wish to utilize them. Such clippings can include examples of deviant behavior, preferably wtih a range of causation and outcome, including some criminal and some "human interest" examples, and so on. Students can look for attributions, implicit personality theories, the medical model, patterns of legal handling of the deivant, and so on.

Chapter 15 Short-Essay Questions

1. Describe the four criteria that may be used for diagnosing or defining abnormal behavior. What are some of the difficulties with each of them?
2. What are some of the personality characteristics considered indicative of normality, or good mental health? Does this mean that only the mentally healthy possess such characteristics?
3. Note three of the common forms of neurosis. Which of these is typically most successful in reducing anxiety? Which is least successful?
4. Describe the manic-depressive psychoses. What is the typical behavior of a patient with such a problem?
5. Compare the psychoanalytic, social learning, and genetic/biochemical theories of depression. How does the concept of vulnerability to accumulated stress help to integrate these views?
6. Describe some of the major behavioral characteristics of those people defined as schizophrenic. What general problem or disturbance can be said to include all of these?
7. What three general factors are suspected as causes of schizophrenia? What evidence is there to implicate each?
8. What characteristics define a psychopathic personality? What hypotheses have been advanced to explain the origins of such behavior, and what research evidence is there to support them?
9. Describe the progression of a person as he or she becomes an alcoholic, touching on possible causes, stages of alcoholism, signs that the person has become an alcoholic, and possibilities of cure.
10. What are some of the difficulties involved in assessing the extent of mental problems in a society, their distribution within it, and any changes over time?

CHAPTER 16: METHODS OF THERAPY

Summary

Chapter 16 gives the history of psychotherapy and the professions involved, then considers three main techniques—psychoanalysis, behavior therapies, and humanistic therapies—with further discussion of group therapy and an eclectic approach. A Critical Discussion considers "mental illness" versus "maladaptive habits" models of mental illness. Problems in assessing the effectiveness of psychotherapy are discussed, followed by coverage of the major biological therapies—electroshock, psychosurgery, and drugs—with a Critical Discussion on the double-blind procedure. It ends with community and personal techniques for promoting mental health.

Chapter 16 Film Suggestions

Abnormal Behavior: A Mental Hospital. CRM. Intended to alert the viewer to the differences between popular myths about mental hospitals and the reality. Shows a series of patient-therapist sessions filmed through one-way windows (with patient consent) at Gateways Mental Hospital in Glendale, California. 28 min. Color. 1971.

An Approach to Growth: Awareness Training. MH. Filmed at the Lomi School in Kauai, Hawaii. Shows a variety of therapies and exercises, such as Hatha Yoga, bioenergetics, rolfing, breathing, kinesthetics, and dreams, as experiences in relaxation and awareness. Depicts some aspects of Gestalt therapy: Subjects are seen talking and acting out their problems in a group. There is, the film asserts, no negative aspect to the search for fuller self-awareness. 26 min. Color. 1973.

Behavior Modification: Teaching Language to Psychotic Children. EMC. Examines Ivar Lovaas' methods of teaching psychotic children aged four to eight the functional use of speech, utilizing operant conditioning. Shows that self-destructive acts must first be suppressed, using punishment, including shock, before the children can learn the simple imitation of speech. Demonstrates teaching the children to understand the meaning of words and to comprehend ideas based on external stimuli. 43 min. Color. 1969.

Behavior Therapy: An Introduction. HR. Shows how operant, classical, and observational models of learning are used by therapists with a variety of problems: a young mother who cannot control her child's increasingly violent tantrums, a college student petrified of giving an oral report in class, and a young man unable to establish meaningful social contacts. Demonstrations of contingency-management, counter-conditioning, and role-playing therapies are provided by Joseph Wolpe, Harry Kalish, and Virginia Roswell. Emphasizes the importance of the client-therapist relationship as well as the philosophy of behavior therapy. 23 min. Color. 1978.

Come Out, Come Out, Whoever You Are. EMC. Nine long-term mental patients, who have become so dependent on their hospital that they do not want to be released, undergo the intensive and controversial "confrontation therapy," in which abnormal behavior is confronted with verbal criticism. Patients who believe themselves to be "crazy" are told to act and talk "crazy," forcing them to examine their behavior. Notes that within six months of this therapy one man spoke for the first time in 23 years and seven of the nine found jobs in the outside world. A moving and provocative film, despite its rather poor production quality. 59 min. Black and white. 1971.

Community of Communities. EMC. Documents an ambitious program in which some 700 college students volunteered to interact with mental patients in board-

and-care homes in San Jose, California. These patients, released when Agnews State Hospital was closed in 1972, had lived in limbo until the student effort. The project won the state award for best mental health project in Santa Clara County. As a result, participants made this informal and honest film to stimulate further community involvement. 23 min. Black and white. 1977.

Cry Help. EMC. Case studies of two adolescents committed to California's Napa State Mental Hospital. Follows two girls through several months of special therapy, emphasizing group discussions and psychodrama classes. Narrated by their group leader, who comments on their progress. Stresses need for enlightened therapy and exposes lack of adequate staff and facilities to handle growing national problem of adolescent mental illness. Award winner. 80 min. Color. 1970.

(*Depression: A Study in Abnormal Behavior*; see Chapter 15.)

Dialogues: Dr. Carl Rogers (Part I). EMC. Wide-ranging interview with the developer of client-oriented therapy and a founder of the human potential movement. Covers motivation, learning, Freudian concepts, development of client-oriented therapy, roles of the client and therapist, and encounter groups. 49 min. Color. 1971. (For Part II, see Chapter 18.)

Journey Into Self. EMC. Dramatic documentary highlights of an intensive 16-hour encounter group session among eight adults, all total strangers to one another. Focuses on four group members, recording the most emotional moments of their interaction. Group is led by Carl Rogers and Richard Farson. Academy Award winner. 47 min. Black and white. 1968.

Madness and Medicine (In two parts). CRM. Investigates the uses in mental institutions of three of the more radical therapies: drugs, electroshock, and psychosurgery. The intent is to "explore these modes—how prevalent they are, who is for them, who is against them, how valid the research is, and how to balance society's needs against the individual's rights." Many psychiatrists and psychologists will find points of contention in this critical evaluation, and even though some points are refuted by psychiatrists and psychobiologists in the film, others may need class clarification. Award winner. Total: 45 min. Color. 1977.

Mental Health: New Frontiers of Sanity. EMC. Documents extent of mental health problems in North America, briefly traces history of mental therapy, and examines two important trends in treatment. One is based on the concept that society causes mental illness; it emphasizes group therapy, community- and family-based treatment, and human growth centers. The other is based on brain chemistry and emphasizes role of drugs, including LSD, in therapy. 22 min. Color. 1971.

(*Observational Learning*; see Chapter 7.)

One Step at a Time: An Introduction to Behavior Modification. CRM. Narrated by Roger Ulrich, who suggests that behavioral techniques are still experimental but offer great promise. Shows techniques of positive reinforcement used in state mental hospital programs, in special school programs, and with the multiply handicapped. 32 min. Color. 1973.

Three Approaches to Psychotherapy (Parts I–III). PCR. A series of three films showing actual footage of the same patient interviewed sequentially by three noted therapists.
Part I: Carl Rogers introduces the series and describes client-centered therapy. 48 min. Black and white. 1968.
Part II: Frederick Perls describes Gestalt therapy. 32 min. Black and white. 1968.
Part III: Albert Ellis describes rational-emotive therapy. 37 min. Black and white. 1968.
(Note: All these films are also available from the maker, Psychological Films, and in color as well as black and white, but the rental cost is substantially higher. Psychological Films also has a new sequel, according to APA, called *Three Approaches to Group Therapy.*)

Token Economy: Behaviorism Applied. CRM. B. F. Skinner discusses the application of his theories in the education and treatment of retardates, criminals, and the mentally ill via the use of tokens in a program of reinforcement therapy. Token economies with retarded and delinquent adolescents are shown and the high success rate of the program is contrasted with the generally lower rehabilitation rate of traditional therapy. 22 min. Color. 1972.

Chapter 16 Lecture/Demonstration Suggestions

The lecture suggestions for Chapters 14 and 15 have already included some that are relevant to Chapter 16. The Chapter 14 discussion noted the problem of disturbed students and suggested ways of guiding them into appropriate therapy; the Chapter 15 discussion included a consideration of the power of labels and referred to David Rosenhan's *Science* article, which is also appropriate here. Also included were notes on the use of case histories, the question of the dangerousness of patients, the complexity of interaction of causation, and the use of newspaper clippings. All of these points are also relevant here, though perhaps in somewhat different ways; the news clippings for Chapter 16, for example, might concern mental hospitals versus community care, and so on.

A useful way to structure the Chapter 16 material is to arrange the issues of psychotherapy as a multi-part question: Who does what to whom, why, and how successfully? You can then add comments or emphasize text material as you wish, at appropriate points. "Who" can include the differences between psychiatrist, psychoanalyst, and psychologist, as well as comments on social workers or non-professionals—for example, anyone from clergy to special cultural categories such as medicine men. A clipping from *Time* (12 June 1972, p. 68), for example, notes a NIMH grant for scholarships for apprentice Navaho medicine men as mental health workers.

"What," of course, involves techniques. "Whom" can be usefully broken into voluntary and involuntary patients, the latter including criminals as well as those whose noncriminal deviant behavior has led to sanctions. "Why" can include these deviance-leading-to-sanction issues but is primarily intended to imply the relation of particular theories to practices. A useful book for this purpose, as well as for the ethical issues noted below, is Perry London's *The Modes and Morals of Psychotherapy* (New York: Holt, Rinehart & Winston, 1964). He points out nicely the somewhat complex relationships involved—for example, that more than one theory can lead to a particular technique and that the effectiveness of a technique is not "proof" of the theory that led to it.

The "how successfully" issue is complex, an issue that the text treats (pp. 506–08) but that can easily be elaborated further, if you wish. You can, for example, expand the point that neither "satisfied patients" nor "satisfied therapists" are very meaningful measures of the utility of a given therapy (p. 506). Reasons for patients' beliefs being of limited use include selection bias, "spontaneous" recovery, unknown influences of other people and events, placebo effects, the Hawthorne effect, and the "hello-goodbye effect." For the therapist, problems include attribution errors (for example, "I helped that one but the other one got worse despite my help") and other dissonance effects based on the therapist's tremendous investment of money, time, and energy—in addition to the fact that information from patients may be biased, by the factors noted earlier.

The same problems can be related to the difficulty in obtaining better answers to the question of therapeutic success. Research is made technically very difficult by many factors, of course. But, in addition, the same tendencies to believe in their own therapies make therapists reluctant to "withhold treatment," in order to get long-term control groups.

The question of control groups is an ethical issue, one that is, in fact, embedded in a matrix of ethical questions. While coverage of the other material may leave little time for this, it is worth noting the type and extent of such questions. It is important to realize, for example, the extent to which therapists' theoretical views of personality and its problems influence their views of what the ethical *questions* are, as well as the answers. London's *The Modes and Morals of Psychotherapy* (noted above) is a good source for these issues. Most of your students, for example, are likely to see behavior modification as manipulative and ethically questionable. But, as London points out, therapists who use it tend to do so for limited problems and those defined by their patients. (This is true for voluntary patients, at least; the ethics of involuntary patients involve different issues. Skinner's view of the latter is presented in "The Ethics of Helping People," *The Humanist*, January/February 1976. This article is also included as a selection in his recent book *Reflections on Behaviorism and Society*, Englewood Cliffs, N.J.: Prentice-Hall, 1978.) To redefine the patient's problem as a deeper and more long-term one requiring a modification of the whole personality, as a psychoanalyst might do, can be argued to be *more* manipulative and also open to serious ethical objection. (As in many areas of introductory psychology, your own beliefs will determine how you view these issues, but fairness to students would dictate that the existing arguments be explored, as part of a general introduction to psychology.)

Chapter 16 Short-Essay Questions

1. Discuss some of the major events in the history of the treatment of the mentally ill that foreshadowed or led to modern procedures.
2. Note the four major categories of mental health professionals, including the training and typical duties of each.
3. Describe the major therapeutic procedures and concepts of psychoanalysis as a technique of psychotherapy.
4. Describe the major therapeutic procedures and concepts of behavior therapy.
5. Describe the major therapeutic procedures and concepts of client-centered psychotherapy.
6. What is meant by symptom substitution, and why is this question important in the "mental illness" versus "maladaptive habits" controversy?
7. What are some of the major advantages of group therapy? What disadvantages have arisen from the expansion of such procedures to encounter groups, sensitivity groups, and so on?
8. Why is it difficult to assess the relative effectiveness of different types of psychotherapy?
9. What are biological therapies? Include several specific types and compare their effectiveness.
10. What techniques can be used to help promote normal emotional development?

CHAPTER 17: SOCIAL PSYCHOLOGY

Summary

Chapter 17 begins with the emphasis on situational influences and phenomenology that characterize social psychology, using bystander intervention as an example. It then considers three main areas of social psychology, beginning with social influence, where the Patty Hearst case is used as a focus. Social perception and the attribution process follow, with Critical Discussions on when two theories compete and the power of labels.

Chapter 17 Film Suggestions

Conformity and Independence. HR. Presents social psychology's main findings in these areas, using both field and laboratory settings. Includes Sherif's experiments on norm formation, Asch's and Milgram's experiments, and others. One of a series by Stanley Milgram. Award winner. 23 min. Color.

Eye of the Storm. EMC. A film of a two-day experiment in which children in a third-grade class were identified as "superior" or "inferior" on the basis of their eye color and promptly demonstrated the viciousness of prejudice. Even the schoolwork of the "inferior" children suffered. When they changed roles the next day, their feelings and treatment of each other changed correspondingly. Award winner. 26 min. Color. 1970.

Group Dynamics: "Groupthink." CRM. Irving L. Janis analyzes what he calls "groupthink," characterized by such factors as the illusion of unanimity, direct pressure on a deviant member, and mind guarding—a device to protect the group from dissenting opinions. Janis uses several historical instances, including President Kennedy's handling of the Cuban missile crisis, to demonstrate how effective leadership can prevent a decision-making group from falling into "groupthink." 22 min. Color. 1973.

(*Human Aggression*; see Chapter 11.)

Invisible Walls. EMC. Focuses on personal space, showing that people encase themselves in invisible walls about 18 inches from their bodies and that violation of these imaginary walls causes a feeling of discomfort. An actor and actress randomly stop unsuspecting subjects and, while ostensibly conducting a consumer survey, violate each subject's personal space. Award winner. 12 min. Black and white. 1969.

Invitation to Social Psychology. HR. Introduces the student to social psychology by focusing on three questions: What is the subject matter? What are its methods of investigation? What are some of its discoveries? Topics covered include classic experiments on affiliation, attribution, cognitive dissonance, conformity, aggression, behavior in a simulated prison, and bystander intervention. One of a series by Stanley Milgram. Winner of several awards. 25 min. Color.

Moral Development. CRM. A re-creation of Stanley Milgram's famous shock studies. David Rosenhan acts as the experimenter; college-age male subjects role-play behavior taken from Milgram's records, but arranged and portrayed to illustrate Lawrence Kohlberg's stages of moral development. The sometimes-conflicting statements and behaviors of the subjects are discussed in terms of Kohlberg's stages and social learning theory. Award winner. 33 min. Color. 1973.

Obedience. EMC. Subjects of Stanley Milgram's experiment on obedience to authority are instructed to administer electric shocks of increasing severity to another person. 44 min. Black and white. 1969.

Social Psychology. CRM. Using the issue of busing of elementary school children, the film explains social comparison theory, shows how attitudes are formed and changed, and theorizes on the nature of racial prejudice. An actual busing situation was filmed and documentary news footage of community reactions to busing in several localities was added; four prominent social psychologists' comments were incorporated. Award winner. 33 min. Color. 1971.

When Will People Help? The Social Psychology of Bystander Intervention. HBJ. Narrated by Daryl J. Bem, who uses bystander intervention as an example of the kind of problem with which social psychologists deal. Introduces the topic with a discussion of the Kitty Genovese murder, then presents reenactments of several experiments that show how social psychologists go about testing their hypotheses. 25 min. Color. 1976.

Chapter 17 Lecture/Demonstration Suggestions

The film *When Will People Help?* referenced above, was specifically designed to complement this chapter. It vividly portrays the problems and research concerning bystander intervention.

The use of Patty Hearst as a topical focus for the social influence material can easily be expanded to consider some other topical problem that students are familiar with, either one that has already happened—for example, the mass murder-suicide at Jonestown in Guyana—or something in the news at the time you lecture. (Some related issues of compliance, and so on, in the Jonestown events were discussed in *Newsweek*, 4 December 1978.)

Another aspect of Chapter 17 that always interests and involves students is Milgram's work. This can be used quite successfully to discuss several important points: not only compliance and the factors controlling it, but also questions of experimental ethics.

Milgram's paper from *Human Relations* ("Some Conditions of Obedience and Disobedience to Authority," *Human Relations* 18, no. 1 (1965): 57–75) gives you much of what you will need. (This is available as a Warner Modular Reprint, No. 655.) For more recent material see his recent book (*Obedience to Authority*, New

York: Harper & Row, 1974) or the excerpt from it published by *Harper's* ("The Perils of Obedience," December 1973, 62–77). More about Milgram himself is presented in an interview in *Psychology Today*, June 1974. One way to use this material is to lead briefly into Milgram by summarizing the development of social psychology after World War II. With Asch you get some important questions, but there was criticism that the relatively weak situation did not reflect the pressures of the real world. At this point, present the problem: On the one hand, the study of small problems via weak situations suffers from and is criticized on the grounds of irrelevance; on the other hand, attempts to examine the type and magnitude of forces operating in the real world run serious ethical and moral risks in manipulating subjects. This obviously leads into Milgram's studies, some of the most dramatic and widely criticized in psychology.

In presenting Milgram, you have several choices. The CRM film *Moral Development* presents the situation very well. If you do not use the film, briefly describe the standard experimental situation. Then put up the coordinates for the percentage of compliant subjects versus voltage level, as in Figure 3 of the *Human Relations* article. Ask your students to guess where the curve first breaks away from total compliance and what percentage of compliance they would expect at the crucial one-third and two-thirds points and at the end. You will have some cynics but most will still guess less than the real data. Before you show them the actual data, also give them the psychiatrists' estimate (also in Figure 3 of the *Human Relations* article).

Give them the actual results. When the reaction dies down a bit, ask them if they think they should believe it and why. Give them the reasons Milgram feels one should believe it. Cover the inevitable questions of the representativeness of the subjects. (The *Harper's* excerpt includes data on replications in other countries—some of which show more compliance than the U.S. results.) Then you can consider the variables that Milgram found important in varying the level of compliance. If you feel that the results seem too pessimistic, point out, as Milgram does, that some people did refuse and that when some refuse, others will follow.

If you have more time, or do not wish to spend so much time on Milgram, you may use Zimbardo's prison study, done at Stanford (*Cognition* 2(2) (1974): 243–56). A slide show on this research is available from Zimbardo, as noted in Section IIC5. Again, a powerful situation yielded striking results in excess of even the experimenter's expectation, and again one result was criticism on ethical grounds.

Chapter 17 Short-Essay Questions

1. Describe the two major features of the social-psychological approach that differentiate it from the rest of psychology.

2. What are the two ways that the presence of several bystanders is said to reduce the probability that any one of them will intervene in an emergency? What factor (other than changing the number of bystanders) will make it *more* likely that they will intervene?
3. What are some of the variations in the Milgram study that yielded lower compliance by subjects? Which one of these variations led to "cheating"?
4. How do the results of the one dollar-twenty dollar experiment and the forbidden-toy experiment support Leon Festinger's theory of cognitive dissonance?
5. Define and explain the function of a reference group, using Patty Hearst and the SLA as an example.
6. When we are given conflicting information about someone, in the form of favorable initial information, say, followed by unfavorable information, under what conditions might we come to think of them unfavorably? Could we be helped to be objective or neutral in our judgment by any procedure?
7. What are some of the factors that have been investigated as possible promoters of interpersonal attraction? Which one of these is more powerful than is usually recognized—or at least admitted?
8. Define the covariance and discounting rules and explain how they function in our interpretation of the behavior of others.
9. Explain how the theory of self-perception would interpret the results of the one dollar-twenty dollar study.
10. Define the fundamental attribution error and discuss some of the effects it may have in social interactions.

CHAPTER 18: PSYCHOLOGY AND SOCIETY

Summary

Chapter 18 considers issues of psychology and society, beginning with prejudice and including stereotypes and a Critical Discussion on sexism. It then considers the influence of mass media, the psychological effects of noise and crowding, and what psychology's role in public policy has been and might be, including a Critical Discussion on scientific jury selection.

Chapter 18 Film Suggestions

Decision. EMC. A fable about personal involvement in social change. Unable to sleep, a man discusses with his wife whether to serve alongside his neighbor. She urges him to stand and be counted, while he feels that he is not needed and there are plenty of others, and he resists the idea of opposing the majority and the establishment. He finally decides to go but feels his action is unimportant. At daybreak we see him emerge—as a Concord minuteman, flintlock in hand. By Xerox. 6 min. Color. 1975.

Dialogues: Dr. Carl Rogers (Part II). EMC. Continues interview, focusing on contemporary issues: American education, student protests, and controversial issues in contemporary psychology, such as action versus research. Rogers also evaluates his contributions to psychology. 51 min. Color. 1971. (For Part I, see Chapter 16.)

(*Moral Development*; see Chapter 17.)

Prejudice: Causes, Consequences, Cures. CRM. Focuses on some of the more interesting and thought-provoking research findings and their implications for dealing with prejudice against women and specific racial, national, and ethnic groups. Explores the damages of stereotypes and their perpetuation by the media, the effects on victims of prejudice, the influence of consciousness-raising groups, and the effects of cooperative contact. 24 min. Color. 1974.

Tilt. CRM. An animated discussion of one of the world's most pressing social and economic problems: How can the peoples of this world share their wealth to save themselves and their earth from disaster? Using animation and whimsy, proposes three methods of sharing the world's wealth among developed and undeveloped countries, each couched in terms of an encounter between a Rich Man, a Poor Man, and a Loaf of Bread. Questions of responsibilities, priorities, and inequities in world ecology, resources, population, international relations, development, wealth, and armaments are explored, although no specific conclusions are drawn. 20 min. Color. 1973.

(*When Will People Help? The Social Psychology of Bystander Intervention*; see Chapter 17.)

Chapter 18 Lecture/Demonstration Suggestions

Chapter 18's orientation to the "real world" and the reciprocal influences between it and the world of psychologists lends itself to lecture and discussion on similar issues. If you watch the newspaper for a week or two before the class, you should be able to find one or more good clippings, and perhaps an ongoing controversy, illustrating one or both directions of influence. You may wish to involve students in the same occupation and then let them offer clippings also. This will help them

162

to become sensitized, as the course draws to a close, to the relationship of psychology and society—the topic of Chapter 18.

If you have asked students to look up original research papers—for example, to familiarize them with *Psychological Abstracts*—you might ask them to mention articles that they read that illustrate one or the other directions of influence.

In connection with this topic you may also wish to point out, or repeat if you have already discussed, the existence and influence of implicit personality theories. These—often "pop-neo-Freud" in content—are remarkably pervasive and subtly influential. (Discussions in nonpsychology media of aggression and TV, for example, often revolve around whether "catharsis" or "modeling" is the most relevant concept—without either being explicitly stated or labeled.)

A closely related topic, of course, that can also be integrated into the same session is the similarly subtle and pervasive influence of sexist ideas and training—that which Bem and Bem have called an "unconscious ideology" ("Homogenizing the American Woman: The Power of an Unconscious Ideology," in *Psychology for Our Times*, 2nd ed., eds. P. Zimbardo and C. Maslach, Glenview, Ill.: Scott, Foresman, 1977). One of the exercises in the *Study Guide* is designed to demonstrate this, based on a procedure of Bem's (described in the text, p. 549). If you have not used the *Study Guide* in your course, you may wish to integrate this technique into your approach. (Essentially, it consists of substituting, in a description, male pronouns and names for female ones and vice versa; only if the result seems perfectly acceptable was the original nonsexist. See the *Study Guide* or p. 549 of the text for further discussion.)

Chapter 18 Short-Essay Questions

1. Compare useful and "working stereotypes" with negative stereotypes that yield prejudice.
2. Discuss the contact hypothesis of prejudice reduction and some of the factors that studies have shown to be helpful in reducing prejudice.
3. Describe the person who would be termed an "authoritarian personality."
4. Discuss the typical results of attempts to change prejudice via legislation and court decisions, including the likelihood of "backlash."
5. How effective are persuasive attempts by the mass media? Why are they not more effective than they are?
6. Describe the Stanford Heart Disease Prevention Program. What does it tell us about the potential effectiveness of the media?
7. Discuss what aspects of environmental noise seem likely to cause problems and what factors help to minimize such problems.
8. Which measure of population density seems to be related to behavioral prob-

lems and which does not? Discuss some of the research that suggests why this might be so.

9. Two U.S. Supreme Court decisions on segregation in education are used in the text to illustrate some points about behavioral science and public policy. In what way was the 1954 decision (against racial segregation in the public schools) similar to the 1896 decision (supporting the "separate but equal" doctrine)? In what way was the 1954 decision different from that of 1896 (other than its findings on the segregation issue)?

10. Where *is* the objectivity of behavioral scientists? *Can* they properly claim to be "doing science" and, if so, why?